CW01336350

The Essential

Tower Air Fryer Cookbook

1500 Days irresistible recipes for beginners, taste the crunchy texture and master the power of the Tower Air Fryer to turn everyday meals into gourmet meals

Angelina J. Broussard

CONTENTS

INTRODUCTION I

How to make the most of your Tower Air Fryer? II
What Tower Air Fryer food collections are offered in this cookbook? II
What changes can the Tower Air Fryer Cookbook make to your diet? III
What are the advantages of the Tower Air Fryer Cookbook for your health? IV

Measurement Conversions VI

Breakfast & Snacks And Fries Recipes 5

Delicious Breakfast Casserole 5
Courgette Fries 5
Egg & Bacon Breakfast Cups 6
Breakfast Doughnuts 6
Avocado Fries 6
Halloumi Fries 7
Cumin Shoestring Carrots 7
Sweet Potato Fries 7
French Toast Slices 8
Mexican Breakfast Burritos 8
Muhammara 9
Potato & Chorizo Frittata 9
Hard Boiled Eggs Air Fryer Style 10
Meaty Egg Cups 10
Cheese Scones 11
Easy Omelette 11
Your Favourite Breakfast Bacon 12
Breakfast "pop Tarts" 12
Polenta Fries 13
Baba Ganoush 13

Sauces & Snack And Appetiser Recipes 14

Cheesy Taco Crescents 14
Tortellini Bites 14
Air-fried Pickles 15
Asian Devilled Eggs 15
Korean Chicken Wings 16
Mini Calzones 16
Pao De Queijo 17
Beetroot Crisps 17
Chicken & Bacon Parcels 17
Scotch Eggs 18
Focaccia Bread 18

Pretzel Bites 19
Jalapeño Pockets 19
Jalapeño Poppers 19
Bacon Smokies 20
Thai Bites 20
Waffle Fries 20
Pasta Chips 21
Onion Bahji 21
Spicy Chickpeas 21

Beef & Lamb And Pork Recipes 22

Cheesy Meatballs 22
Beef Stroganoff 22
Asian Meatballs 23
Lamb Calzone 23
Southern Style Pork Chops 23
Pork Belly With Crackling 24
Cheese & Ham Sliders 24
Air Fryer Pork Bratwurst 24
Steak Popcorn Bites 25
Roast Pork 25
Beef Wellington 25
Italian Meatballs 26
Lamb Burgers 26
Mustard Pork Tenderloin 26
Pulled Pork, Bacon, And Cheese Sliders 27
Breaded Pork Chops 27
Steak Fajitas 28
Mustard Glazed Pork 28
Beef And Cheese Empanadas 29
Pork With Chinese 5 Spice 29

Poultry Recipes 30

Thai Turkey Burgers 30
Bbq Chicken Tenders 30
Crunchy Chicken Tenders 31
Air Fried Maple Chicken Thighs 31
Garlic Parmesan Fried Chicken Wings 32
Chicken Tikka 32
Air Fryer Sesame Chicken Thighs 33
Cornflake Chicken Nuggets 33
Chicken Milanese 34
Turkey Cutlets In Mushroom Sauce 34
Pizza Chicken Nuggets 34
Chicken Fajitas 35
Chicken Kiev 35
Chicken And Cheese Chimichangas 36
Spicy Chicken Wing Drummettes 36

Chicken & Potatoes........ 37
Sticky Chicken Tikka Drumsticks........ 37
Air Fryer Chicken Thigh Schnitzel........ 38
Whole Chicken........ 38
Chicken Tikka Masala........ 39

Fish & Seafood Recipes........ 40

Oat & Parmesan Crusted Fish Fillets........ 40
Lobster Tails........ 40
Traditional Fish And Chips........ 40
Cod Nuggets........ 41
Ranch Style Fish Fillets........ 41
Thai Fish Cakes........ 41
Furikake Salmon........ 42
Copycat Fish Fingers........ 42
Sea Bass With Asparagus Spears........ 43
Tilapia Fillets........ 43
Thai-style Tuna Fishcakes........ 44
Air Fryer Mussels........ 44
Fish Taco Cauliflower Rice Bowls........ 45
Peppery Lemon Shrimp........ 45
Thai Salmon Patties........ 46
Coconut Shrimp........ 46
Shrimp Wrapped With Bacon........ 47
Air Fried Scallops........ 47
Tandoori Salmon........ 48
Crunchy Fish........ 48

Vegetarian & Vegan Recipes........ 49

Jackfruit Taquitos........ 49
Roast Cauliflower & Broccoli........ 49
Artichoke Crostini........ 50
Roast Vegetables........ 50
Whole Wheat Pizza........ 51
Macaroni & Cheese Quiche........ 51
Flat Mushroom Pizzas........ 51
Mushroom Pasta........ 52
Tomato And Herb Tofu........ 52
Roasted Cauliflower........ 53
Parmesan Truffle Oil Fries........ 53
Aubergine Parmigiana........ 53
Falafel Burgers........ 54
Gnocchi Caprese........ 54
Baked Feta, Tomato & Garlic Pasta........ 55
Rainbow Vegetables........ 55
Courgette Burgers........ 55
Radish Hash Browns........ 56
Satay Tofu Skewers........ 56

Air-fried Artichoke Hearts 56

Side Dishes Recipes 57

Zingy Brussels Sprouts 57
Stuffing Filled Pumpkin 57
Hasselback New Potatoes 57
Crispy Sweet & Spicy Cauliflower 58
Alternative Stuffed Potatoes 58
Yorkshire Puddings 58
Aubergine Parmesan 59
Super Easy Fries 59
Air Fryer Corn On The Cob 59
Butternut Squash 60
Roasted Okra 60
Egg Fried Rice 60
Orange Sesame Cauliflower 61
Pumpkin Fries 61
Honey Roasted Parsnips 61
Crispy Broccoli 62
Tex Mex Hash Browns 62
Garlic And Parsley Potatoes 62
Mexican Rice 63
Celery Root Fries 63

Desserts Recipes 64

Christmas Biscuits 64
Chocolate Cake 64
Sugar Dough Dippers 65
Chocolate Orange Muffins 65
Coffee, Chocolate Chip, And Banana Bread 66
Chocolate Eclairs 66
Brownies 67
Chocolate-glazed Banana Slices 67
Peanut Butter And Banana Bites 67
Brazilian Pineapple 68
Apple And Cinnamon Puff Pastry Pies 68
Milk And White Chocolate Chip Air Fryer Donuts With Frosting 69
Spiced Apples 69
Granola 70
Butter Cake 70
Pistachio Brownies 71
New York Cheesecake 71
Zebra Cake 72
Grilled Ginger & Coconut Pineapple Rings 72
Special Oreos 72

Appendix : Recipes Index 73

INTRODUCTION

Welcome to the tantalizing world of the Tower Air Fryer-shell 15-UK01. As a passionate food lover and devoted home cook, I am thrilled to present to you "The Essential Tower Air Fryer Cookbook." My name is Angelina J. Broussard, and I am delighted to be your guide on this delectable journey.

Prepare to embark on a gastronomic adventure like no other, as we explore the incredible capabilities of the Tower Air Fryer and discover a world of delicious possibilities. This cookbook has been carefully crafted to inspire and elevate your cooking experience, ensuring that every meal you prepare becomes a masterpiece.

Within the pages of this cookbook, you will find a treasure trove of recipes that showcase the versatility and convenience of the Tower Air Fryer. From crispy appetizers that will tantalize your taste buds to succulent main courses that will have your family and friends begging for seconds, this collection offers a diverse range of culinary delights.

But this cookbook is more than just a compilation of recipes—it is a guide to mastering the art of air frying. Join me as we delve into the nuances of this remarkable appliance, discovering its optimal temperature settings, cooking times, and innovative techniques. Together, we will unlock the secrets to achieving that perfect golden crispness while maintaining the juiciness and flavors of your favorite dishes.

So, fellow food enthusiasts, get ready to embark on a culinary adventure that will take your taste buds on a remarkable journey. Embrace the sizzle, the aromas, and the joy that cooking with the Tower Air Fryer brings. Let "The Essential Tower Air Fryer Cookbook" be your trusted guide as you unlock the full potential of this extraordinary appliance and create culinary masterpieces that will impress your loved ones.

It is my utmost pleasure to be your companion in this exciting culinary voyage. May this cookbook inspire you to explore, create, and savor the delights that await you in the realm of the Tower Air Fryer.

Happy cooking!

How to make the most of your Tower Air Fryer?

To make the most of your Tower Air Fryer and fully enjoy its benefits, consider the following tips:

- **Explore Air Fryer Recipes:** To fully utilize your Tower Air Fryer, explore air fryer recipes available online or invest in a dedicated air fryer cookbook. These resources can provide inspiration, tips, and guidance on how to make the most of your appliance.

- **Use the Correct Cooking Temperature:** Different recipes may require different cooking temperatures. It's important to follow the recommended temperature settings provided in the recipe or adjust accordingly based on your desired results. Preheating the air fryer will help achieve the desired temperature faster.

- **Experiment with Different Ingredients:** Don't limit yourself to traditional fried foods. The Tower Air Fryer is versatile and can be used to cook a wide range of ingredients. Experiment with vegetables, proteins, frozen snacks, and even desserts to explore the variety of dishes you can create.

- **Explore Different Recipes and Ingredients:** One of the joys of using an air fryer is the versatility it offers. Experiment with a wide range of recipes and ingredients to discover new flavors and culinary creations. From vegetables and proteins to desserts and snacks, the Tower Air Fryer can accommodate various recipes and allow for creative exploration.

- **Keep an Eye on Food Texture:** As you gain experience with your Tower Air Fryer, pay attention to the texture of the food being cooked. Adjust the cooking time or temperature accordingly to achieve the desired level of crispiness or tenderness.

By following these tips and experimenting with different recipes and ingredients, you can make the most of your Tower Air Fryer and enjoy delicious, crispy, and healthy meals with ease.

What Tower Air Fryer food collections are offered in this cookbook?

In "The Essential Tower Air Fryer Cookbook," you will find a variety of food collections that cater to different tastes and occasions. Here are some examples of the Tower Air Fryer food collections that may be offered in the cookbook:

Crispy Appetizers: This collection features an array of delicious and crispy appetizers, such as crispy chicken wings, mozzarella sticks, onion rings, or loaded potato skins. These recipes are perfect for starting a meal or serving as party snacks.

International Flavors: Explore global cuisine with this collection of recipes inspired by different countries and cultures. You might find air-fried samosas, crispy spring rolls, Greek-style lamb skewers, or even Korean-inspired fried chicken. These recipes offer a culinary adventure right in your kitchen.

Deliciously Sweet Treats: Satisfy your sweet tooth with this collection of dessert recipes specifically created for the Tower Air Fryer. From apple turnovers and churros to cinnamon sugar donut holes or berry-filled hand pies, these recipes showcase how the air fryer can create delectable, crispy desserts.

Comfort Food Classics: Indulge in nostalgic comfort foods made healthier with the Tower Air Fryer. This collection may include recipes for crispy chicken schnitzel, mac and cheese bites, sweet potato fries, or even air-fried donuts. Enjoy your favorite comfort foods with a guilt-free twist.

Healthy Veggie Delights: This collection focuses on using the Tower Air Fryer to prepare a variety of healthy and flavorful vegetable dishes. From crispy zucchini fries to roasted Brussels sprouts or stuffed bell peppers, these recipes showcase the versatility of the air fryer for creating nutritious vegetarian options.

Please note that the specific food collections in "The Essential Tower Air Fryer Cookbook" may vary. The cookbook is designed to offer a diverse range of recipes to cater to different tastes, dietary preferences, and culinary interests, ensuring there is something for everyone to enjoy.

What changes can the Tower Air Fryer Cookbook make to your diet?

The Tower Air Fryer Cookbook can bring about several positive changes to your diet. Here are some ways in which incorporating air frying into your cooking routine using the recipes from the cookbook can make a difference:

- **Healthier Cooking Method:** The Tower Air Fryer utilizes hot air circulation to cook food, requiring significantly less oil compared to traditional frying methods. By air frying, you can reduce the amount of unhealthy fats and calories in your meals, promoting a healthier diet overall.

- **Reduced Consumption of Deep-Fried Foods:** Deep-fried foods are often associated with high calorie, fat, and sodium content. With the Tower Air Fryer Cookbook, you can still enjoy the crispy texture and delicious flavors of your favorite fried foods without the excess oil and calories. This can help reduce your consumption of deep-fried foods, leading to a more balanced and nutritious diet.

- **Increased Vegetable Intake:** The Tower Air Fryer Cookbook offers a variety of vegetable-focused recipes that are both delicious and nutritious. By incorporating more air-fried vegetables into your meals, you can increase your intake of vitamins, minerals, and dietary fiber. It encourages you to explore different vegetable dishes and experiment with flavors, making it easier to incorporate more plant-based foods into your diet.

- **Less Processed Food Consumption:** Air frying allows you to prepare homemade versions of traditionally deep-fried processed foods, such as French fries or chicken nuggets, using fresh ingredients. By making these foods at home with the Tower Air Fryer, you can have more control over the quality of ingredients, reduce your intake of preservatives and additives, and opt for healthier alternatives.

- **Cooking at Home:** Using the Tower Air Fryer Cookbook encourages cooking at home, allowing you to have control over the ingredients, portion sizes, and cooking methods. By preparing meals at home, you can reduce your reliance on processed and restaurant foods, which often contain higher levels of unhealthy fats, sodium, and added sugars.

What are the advantages of the Tower Air Fryer Cookbook for your health?

"The Tower Air Fryer Cookbook" offers several advantages for your health:

- **Reduced Oil and Fat** Intake: One of the primary health benefits of using the Tower Air Fryer Cookbook is the significant reduction in oil and fat consumption. Air frying allows you to achieve a crispy texture and delicious flavors with minimal oil compared to traditional frying methods. By using less oil, you can lower your intake of unhealthy fats and calories, which can contribute to maintaining a healthier weight and reducing the risk of cardiovascular diseases.

- **Increased Intake of Nutritious Foods:** "The Tower Air Fryer Cookbook" encourages the inclusion of vegetables, lean proteins, whole grains, and other nutritious ingredients in your meals. By following the cookbook's recipes, you can increase your intake of essential vitamins, minerals, and dietary fiber, supporting overall health and well-being.

• **Encourages Balanced and Varied Meals:** "The Tower Air Fryer Cookbook" offers a wide range of recipes that promote balanced and varied meals. By incorporating different types of proteins, vegetables, grains, and fruits into your diet, you can ensure that you receive a diverse array of essential nutrients. This helps support overall health and provides the body with the necessary vitamins, minerals, and antioxidants it needs to function optimally.

• **Promotion of Home Cooking:** Using the Tower Air Fryer Cookbook encourages more home cooking, which is generally associated with healthier food choices. When you prepare meals at home, you have control over the ingredients, portion sizes, and cooking methods. This can lead to a reduction in the consumption of processed foods, added sugars, and unhealthy additives often found in pre-packaged or takeout meals.

While "The Tower Air Fryer Cookbook" offers health-conscious recipes and promotes healthier cooking methods, it's important to note that individual dietary choices and overall lifestyle factors also play a crucial role in maintaining good health. A balanced and varied diet, regular physical activity, and other healthy habits are essential components of a healthy lifestyle.

Measurement Conversions

BASIC KITCHEN CONVERSIONS & EQUIVALENTS

DRY MEASUREMENTS CONVERSION CHART

3 TEASPOONS = 1 TABLESPOON = 1/16 CUP

6 TEASPOONS = 2 TABLESPOONS = 1/8 CUP

12 TEASPOONS = 4 TABLESPOONS = 1/4 CUP

24 TEASPOONS = 8 TABLESPOONS = 1/2 CUP

36 TEASPOONS = 12 TABLESPOONS = 3/4 CUP

48 TEASPOONS = 16 TABLESPOONS = 1 CUP

METRIC TO US COOKING CONVERSIONS

OVEN TEMPERATURES

120 °C = 250 °F

160 °C = 320 °F

180° C = 350 °F

205 °C = 400 °F

220 °C = 425 °F

LIQUID MEASUREMENTS CONVERSION CHART

8 FLUID OUNCES = 1 CUP = 1/2 PINT = 1/4 QUART

16 FLUID OUNCES = 2 CUPS = 1 PINT = 1/2 QUART

32 FLUID OUNCES = 4 CUPS = 2 PINTS = 1 QUART

= 1/4 GALLON

128 FLUID OUNCES = 16 CUPS = 8 PINTS = 4 QUARTS = 1 GALLON

BAKING IN GRAMS

1 CUP FLOUR = 140 GRAMS

1 CUP SUGAR = 150 GRAMS

1 CUP POWDERED SUGAR = 160 GRAMS

1 CUP HEAVY CREAM = 235 GRAMS

VOLUME

1 MILLILITER = 1/5 TEASPOON

5 ML = 1 TEASPOON

15 ML = 1 TABLESPOON

240 ML = 1 CUP OR 8 FLUID OUNCES

1 LITER = 34 FL. OUNCES

WEIGHT

1 GRAM = .035 OUNCES

100 GRAMS = 3.5 OUNCES

500 GRAMS = 1.1 POUNDS

1 KILOGRAM = 35 OUNCES

US TO METRIC COOKING CONVERSIONS

1/5 TSP = 1 ML

1 TSP = 5 ML

1 TBSP = 15 ML

1 FL OUNCE = 30 ML

1 CUP = 237 ML

1 PINT (2 CUPS) = 473 ML

1 QUART (4 CUPS) = .95 LITER

1 GALLON (16 CUPS) = 3.8 LITERS

1 OZ = 28 GRAMS

1 POUND = 454 GRAMS

BUTTER

1 CUP BUTTER = 2 STICKS = 8 OUNCES = 230 GRAMS = 8 TABLESPOONS

WHAT DOES 1 CUP EQUAL

1 CUP = 8 FLUID OUNCES

1 CUP = 16 TABLESPOONS

1 CUP = 48 TEASPOONS

1 CUP = 1/2 PINT

1 CUP = 1/4 QUART

1 CUP = 1/16 GALLON

1 CUP = 240 ML

BAKING PAN CONVERSIONS

1 CUP ALL-PURPOSE FLOUR = 4.5 OZ

1 CUP ROLLED OATS = 3 OZ 1 LARGE EGG = 1.7 OZ

1 CUP BUTTER = 8 OZ 1 CUP MILK = 8 OZ

1 CUP HEAVY CREAM = 8.4 OZ

1 CUP GRANULATED SUGAR = 7.1 OZ

1 CUP PACKED BROWN SUGAR = 7.75 OZ

1 CUP VEGETABLE OIL = 7.7 OZ

1 CUP UNSIFTED POWDERED SUGAR = 4.4 OZ

BAKING PAN CONVERSIONS

9-INCH ROUND CAKE PAN = 12 CUPS

10-INCH TUBE PAN =16 CUPS

11-INCH BUNDT PAN = 12 CUPS

9-INCH SPRINGFORM PAN = 10 CUPS

9 X 5 INCH LOAF PAN = 8 CUPS

9-INCH SQUARE PAN = 8 CUPS

Breakfast & Snacks And Fries Recipes

Delicious Breakfast Casserole

Servings: 4
Cooking Time:xx

Ingredients:

- 4 frozen hash browns
- 8 sausages, cut into pieces
- 4 eggs
- 1 diced yellow pepper
- 1 diced green pepper
- 1 diced red pepper
- Half a diced onion

Directions:

1. Line the bottom of your fryer with aluminium foil and arrange the hash browns inside
2. Add the sausage on top (uncooked)
3. Now add the onions and the peppers, sprinkling evenly
4. Cook the casserole on 170ºC for around 10 minutes
5. Open your fryer and give the mixture a good stir
6. Combine the eggs in a small bowl and pour over the casserole, closing the lid
7. Cook for another 10 minutes on the same temperature
8. Serve with a little seasoning to taste

Courgette Fries

Servings: 2
Cooking Time:xx

Ingredients:

- 1 courgette/zucchini
- 3 tablespoons plain/all-purpose flour (gluten-free if you wish)
- ¼ teaspoon salt
- ¼ teaspoon freshly ground black pepper
- 60 g/¾ cup dried breadcrumbs (gluten-free if you wish; see page 9)
- 1 teaspoon dried oregano
- 20 g/¼ cup finely grated Parmesan
- 1 egg, beaten

Directions:

1. Preheat the air-fryer to 180ºC/350ºF.
2. Slice the courgette/zucchini into fries about 1.5 x 1.5 x 5 cm/⅝ x ⅝ x 2 in.
3. Season the flour with salt and pepper. Combine the breadcrumbs with the oregano and Parmesan.
4. Dip the courgettes/zucchini in the flour (shaking off any excess flour), then the egg, then the seasoned breadcrumbs.
5. Add the fries to the preheated air-fryer and air-fry for 15 minutes. They should be crispy on the outside but soft on the inside. Serve immediately.

Egg & Bacon Breakfast Cups

Servings: 8
Cooking Time:xx

Ingredients:

- 6 eggs
- 1 chopped red pepper
- 1 chopped green pepper
- 1 chopped yellow pepper
- 2 tbsp double cream
- 50g chopped spinach
- 50g grated cheddar cheese
- 50g grated mozzarella cheese
- 3 slices of cooked bacon, crumbled into pieces

Directions:

1. Take a large mixing bowl and crack the eggs
2. Add the cream and season with a little salt and pepper, combining everything well
3. Add the peppers, spinach, onions, both cheeses, and the crumbled bacon, combining everything once more
4. You will need silicone moulds or cups for this part, and you should pour equal amounts of the mixture into 8 cups
5. Cook at 150ºC for around 12 or 15 minutes, until the eggs are cooked properly

Breakfast Doughnuts

Servings: 4
Cooking Time:xx

Ingredients:

- 1 packet of Pillsbury Grands
- 5 tbsp raspberry jam
- 1 tbsp melted butter
- 5 tbsp sugar

Directions:

1. Preheat your air fryer to 250ºC
2. Place the Pillsbury Grands into the air fryer and cook for around 5m minutes
3. Remove and place to one side
4. Take a large bowl and add the sugar
5. Coat the doughnuts in the melted butter, coating evenly
6. Dip into the sugar and coat evenly once more
7. Using an icing bag, add the jam into the bag and pipe an even amount into each doughnut
8. Eat warm or cold

Avocado Fries

Servings: 2
Cooking Time:xx

Ingredients:

- 35 g/¼ cup plain/all-purpose flour (gluten free if you wish)
- ½ teaspoon chilli/chili powder
- 1 egg, beaten
- 50 g/heaped ½ cup dried breadcrumbs (gluten-free if you wish; see page 9)
- 1 avocado, skin and stone removed, and each half sliced lengthways
- salt and freshly ground black pepper

Directions:

1. Preheat the air-fryer to 200ºC/400ºF.
2. In a bowl combine the flour and chilli/chili powder, then season with salt and pepper. Place the beaten egg in a second bowl and the breadcrumbs in a third bowl.
3. Dip each avocado slice in the seasoned flour (shaking off any excess), then the egg and finally the breadcrumbs.
4. Add the breaded avocado slices to the preheated air-fryer and air-fry for 6 minutes, turning after 4 minutes. Serve immediately.

Halloumi Fries

Servings: 2
Cooking Time:xx

Ingredients:

- 225 g/8 oz. halloumi
- 40 g/heaped ¼ cup plain/all-purpose flour (gluten-free if you wish)
- ½ teaspoon sweet smoked paprika
- ½ teaspoon dried oregano
- ¼ teaspoon mild chilli/chili powder
- olive oil or avocado oil, for spraying

Directions:

1. Preheat the air-fryer to 180ºC/350ºF.
2. Slice the halloumi into fries roughly 2 x 1.5 cm/¾ x ⅝ in.
3. Mix the flour and seasoning in a bowl and dip each halloumi stick into the flour to coat. Spray with a little oil.
4. Add the fries to the preheated air-fryer and air-fry for 5 minutes. Serve immediately.

Cumin Shoestring Carrots

Servings: 2
Cooking Time:xx

Ingredients:

- 300 g/10½ oz. carrots
- 1 teaspoon cornflour/cornstarch
- 1 teaspoon ground cumin
- ¼ teaspoon salt
- 1 tablespoon olive oil
- garlic mayonnaise, to serve

Directions:

1. Preheat the air-fryer to 200ºC/400ºF.
2. Peel the carrots and cut into thin fries, roughly 10 cm x 1 cm x 5 mm/4 x ½ x ¼ in. Toss the carrots in a bowl with all the other ingredients.
3. Add the carrots to the preheated air-fryer and air-fry for 9 minutes, shaking the drawer of the air-fryer a couple of times during cooking. Serve with garlic mayo on the side.

Sweet Potato Fries

Servings: 4
Cooking Time:xx

Ingredients:

- 2 medium sweet potatoes
- 2 teaspoons olive oil
- ½ teaspoon salt
- ½ teaspoon chilli/hot red pepper flakes
- ½ teaspoon smoked paprika

Directions:

1. Preheat the air-fryer to 190ºC/375ºF.
2. Peel the sweet potatoes and slice into fries about 1 x 1 cm/½ x ½ in. by the length of the potato. Toss the sweet potato fries in the oil, salt, chilli and paprika, making sure every fry is coated.
3. Tip into the preheated air-fryer in a single layer (you may need to cook them in two batches, depending on the size of your air-fryer). Air-fry for 10 minutes, turning once halfway during cooking. Serve immediately.

French Toast Slices

Servings: 1
Cooking Time:xx

Ingredients:

- 2 eggs
- 5 slices sandwich bread
- 100ml milk
- 2 tbsp flour
- 3 tbsp sugar
- 1 tsp ground cinnamon
- 1/2 tsp vanilla extract
- Pinch of salt

Directions:

1. Preheat your air fryer to 220ºC
2. Take your bread and cut it into three pieces of the same size
3. Take a mixing bowl and combine the other ingredients until smooth
4. Dip the bread into the mixture, coating evenly
5. Take a piece of parchment paper and lay it inside the air fryer
6. Arrange the bread on the parchment paper in one layer
7. Cook for 5 minutes
8. Turn and cook for another 5 minutes

Mexican Breakfast Burritos

Servings: 6
Cooking Time:xx

Ingredients:

- 6 scrambled eggs
- 6 medium tortillas
- Half a minced red pepper
- 8 sausages, cut into cubes and browned
- 4 pieces of bacon, pre-cooked and cut into pieces
- 65g grated cheese of your choice
- A small amount of olive oil for cooking

Directions:

1. Into a regular mixing bowl, combine the eggs, bell pepper, bacon pieces, the cheese, and the browned sausage, giving everything a good stir
2. Take your first tortilla and place half a cup of the mixture into the middle, folding up the top and bottom and rolling closed
3. Repeat until all your tortillas have been used
4. Arrange the burritos into the bottom of your fryer and spray with a little oil
5. Cook the burritos at 170ºC for 5 minutes

Muhammara

Servings: 4
Cooking Time:xx

Ingredients:

- 4 romano peppers
- 4 tablespoons olive oil
- 100 g/1 cup walnuts
- 90 g/1 heaped cup dried breadcrumbs (see page 9)
- 1 teaspoon cumin
- 2 tablespoons pomegranate molasses
- freshly squeezed juice of ½ a lemon
- ½ teaspoon chilli/chili salt (or salt and some chilli/hot red pepper flakes combined)
- fresh pomegranate seeds, to serve

Directions:

1. Preheat the air-fryer to 180ºC/350ºF.
2. Rub the peppers with ½ teaspoon of the olive oil. Add the peppers to the preheated air-fryer and air-fry for 8 minutes.
3. Meanwhile, lightly toast the walnuts by tossing them in a shallow pan over a medium heat for 3–5 minutes. Allow to cool, then grind the walnuts in a food processor. Once the peppers are cooked, chop off the tops and discard most of the seeds. Add to the food processor with all other ingredients. Process until smooth. Allow to cool in the fridge, then serve the dip with pomegranate seeds on top.

Potato & Chorizo Frittata

Servings: 2
Cooking Time:xx

Ingredients:

- 3 eggs
- 1 sliced chorizo sausage
- 1 potato, boiled and cubed
- 50g feta cheese
- 50g frozen sweetcorn
- A pinch of salt
- 1 tbsp olive oil

Directions:

1. Add a little olive oil to the frying basket
2. Add the corn, potato, and sliced chorizo to the basket
3. Cook at 180ºC until the sausage is a little brown
4. In a small bowl, beat together the eggs with a little seasoning
5. Pour the eggs into the pan
6. Crumble the feta on top
7. Cook for 5 minutes
8. Remove and serve in slices

Hard Boiled Eggs Air Fryer Style

Servings: 2
Cooking Time:xx

Ingredients:

- 4 large eggs
- 1 tsp cayenne pepper
- Salt and pepper for seasoning

Directions:

1. Preheat the air fryer to 220ºC
2. Take a wire rack and place inside the air fryer
3. Lay the eggs on the rack
4. Cook for between 15-17 minutes, depending upon how you like your eggs
5. Remove from the fryer and place in a bowl of cold water for around 5 minutes
6. Peel and season with the cayenne and the salt and pepper

Meaty Egg Cups

Servings: 4
Cooking Time:xx

Ingredients:

- 8 slices of toasted sandwich bread
- 2 slices of ham
- 4 eggs
- Salt and pepper to taste
- Butter for greasing

Directions:

1. Take 4 ramekins and grease the insides with a little butter
2. Flatten the slices of toast with a rolling pin and arrange inside the ramekins - two in each
3. Line the inside of each ramekin with a slice of ham
4. Crack one egg into each ramekin
5. Season with a little salt and pepper
6. Place the ramekins into the air fryer and cook at 160ºC for 15 minutes
7. Remove from the fryer and wait to cool just slightly
8. Remove and serve

Cheese Scones

Servings:12
Cooking Time:xx
Ingredients:

- ½ teaspoon baking powder
- 210 g/1½ cups self-raising/self-rising flour (gluten-free if you wish), plus extra for dusting
- 50 g/3½ tablespoons cold butter, cubed
- 125 g/1½ cups grated mature Cheddar
- a pinch of cayenne pepper
- a pinch of salt
- 100 ml/7 tablespoons milk, plus extra for brushing the tops of the scones

Directions:

1. Mix the baking powder with the flour in a bowl, then add the butter and rub into the flour to form a crumblike texture. Add the cheese, cayenne pepper and salt and stir. Then add the milk, a little at a time, and bring together into a ball of dough.
2. Dust your work surface with flour. Roll the dough flat until about 1.5 cm/⅝ in. thick. Cut out the scones using a 6-cm/2½-in. diameter cookie cutter. Gather the offcuts into a ball, re-roll and cut more scones – you should get about 12 scones from the mixture. Place the scones on an air-fryer liner or a piece of pierced parchment paper.
3. Preheat the air-fryer to 180ºC/350ºF.
4. Add the scones to the preheated air-fryer and air-fry for 8 minutes, turning them over halfway to cook the other side. Remove and allow to cool a little, then serve warm.

Easy Omelette

Servings: 1
Cooking Time:xx
Ingredients:

- 50ml milk
- 2 eggs
- 60g grated cheese, any you like
- Any garnishes you like, such as mushrooms, peppers, etc.

Directions:

1. Take a small mixing bowl and crack the eggs inside, whisking with the milk
2. Add the salt and garnishes and combine again
3. Grease a 6x3" pan and pour the mixture inside
4. Arrange the pan inside the air fryer basket
5. Cook at 170ºC for 10 minutes
6. At the halfway point, sprinkle the cheese on top
7. Loosen the edges with a spatula before serving

Your Favourite Breakfast Bacon

Servings: 2
Cooking Time:xx

Ingredients:

- 4-5 rashers of lean bacon, fat cut off
- Salt and pepper for seasoning

Directions:

1. Line your air fryer basket with parchment paper
2. Place the bacon in the basket
3. Set the fryer to 200ºC
4. Cook for 10 minutes for crispy. If you want it very crispy, cook for another 2 minutes

Breakfast "pop Tarts"

Servings: 6
Cooking Time:xx

Ingredients:

- 2 slices of prepared pie crust, shortbread or filo will work fine
- 2 tbsp strawberry jam
- 60ml plain yogurt
- 1 tsp cornstarch
- 1 tsp Stevia sweetener
- 2 tbsp cream cheese
- A drizzle of olive oil

Directions:

1. Lay your pie crust flat and cut into 6 separate rectangular pieces
2. In a small bowl, mix together the cornstarch and the jam
3. Spread 1 tablespoon of the mixture on top of the crust
4. Fold each crust over to form the tart
5. Seal down the edges using a fork
6. Arrange your tarts inside the frying basket and spray with a little olive oil
7. Heat to 175ºC and cook for 10 minutes
8. Meanwhile, combine the yogurt, cream cheese and Stevia in a bowl
9. Remove the tarts and allow to cool
10. Once cool, add the frosting on top and sprinkle with the sugar sprinkles

Polenta Fries

Servings: 6

Cooking Time:xx

Ingredients:

- 800 ml/scant 3½ cups water
- 1½ vegetable stock cubes
- ¾ teaspoon dried oregano
- ¾ teaspoon freshly ground black pepper
- 200 g/1⅓ cups quick-cook polenta/cornmeal
- 2 teaspoons olive oil
- 55 g/6 tablespoons plain/all-purpose flour (gluten-free if you wish)
- garlic mayonnaise, to serve

Directions:

1. Bring the water and stock cubes to the boil in a saucepan with the oregano and black pepper. Stir in the polenta/cornmeal and continue to stir until the mixture becomes significantly more solid and is hard to stir – this should take about 5–6 minutes.
2. Grease a 15 x 15-cm/6 x 6-in. baking pan with some of the olive oil. Tip the polenta into the baking pan, smoothing down with the back of a wet spoon. Leave to cool at room temperature for about 30 minutes, then pop into the fridge for at least an hour.
3. Remove the polenta from the fridge and carefully tip out onto a chopping board. Slice the polenta into fingers 7.5 x 1 x 2 cm/3 x ½ x ¾ in. Roll the polenta fingers in the flour, then spray or drizzle the remaining olive oil over the fingers.
4. Preheat the air-fryer to 200ºC/400ºF.
5. Lay the fingers apart from one another in a single layer in the preheated air-fryer (you may need to cook these in batches, depending on the size of your air-fryer). Air-fry for 9 minutes, turning once halfway through cooking. Serve immediately with garlic mayonnaise.

Baba Ganoush

Servings: 4

Cooking Time:xx

Ingredients:

- 1 large aubergine/eggplant, sliced in half lengthways
- ½ teaspoon salt
- 5 tablespoons olive oil
- 1 bulb garlic
- 30 g/2 tablespoons tahini or nut butter
- 2 tablespoons freshly squeezed lemon juice
- ½ teaspoon ground cumin
- ¼ teaspoon smoked paprika
- salt and freshly ground black pepper
- 3 tablespoons freshly chopped flat-leaf parsley

Directions:

1. Preheat the air-fryer to 200ºC/400ºF.
2. Lay the aubergine/eggplant halves cut side up. Sprinkle over the salt, then drizzle over 1 tablespoon of oil. Cut the top off the garlic bulb, brush the exposed cloves with a little olive oil, then wrap in foil. Place the aubergine/eggplant and foil-wrapped garlic in the preheated air-fryer and air-fry for 15–20 minutes until the inside of the aubergine is soft and buttery in texture.
3. Scoop the flesh of the aubergine into a bowl. Squeeze out about 1 tablespoon of the cooked garlic and add to the bowl with the remaining 4 tablespoons of olive oil, the tahini/nut butter, lemon juice, spices and salt and pepper to taste. Mix well and serve with fresh flat-leaf parsley sprinkled over.

Sauces & Snack And Appetiser Recipes

Cheesy Taco Crescents

Servings: 8
Cooking Time:xx

Ingredients:

- 1 can Pillsbury crescent sheets, or alternative
- 4 Monterey Jack cheese sticks
- 150g browned minced beef
- ½ pack taco seasoning mix

Directions:

1. Preheat the air fryer to 200°C
2. Combine the minced beef and the taco seasoning, warm in the microwave for about 2 minutes
3. Cut the crescent sheets into 8 equal squares
4. Cut the cheese sticks in half
5. Add half a cheese stick to each square, and 2 tablespoons of mince
6. Roll up the dough and pinch at the ends to seal
7. Place in the air fryer and cook for 5 minutes
8. Turnover and cook for another 3 minutes

Tortellini Bites

Servings: 6
Cooking Time:xx

Ingredients:

- 200g cheese tortellini
- 150g flour
- 100g panko bread crumbs
- 50g grated parmesan
- 1 tsp dried oregano
- 2 eggs
- ½ tsp garlic powder
- ½ tsp chilli flakes
- Salt
- Pepper

Directions:

1. Cook the tortellini according to the packet instructions
2. Mix the panko, parmesan, oregano, garlic powder, chilli flakes salt and pepper in a bowl
3. Beat the eggs in another bowl and place the flour in a third bowl
4. Coat the tortellini in flour, then egg and then in the panko mix
5. Place in the air fryer and cook at 185°C for 10 minutes until crispy
6. Serve with marinara sauce for dipping

Air-fried Pickles

Servings: 4
Cooking Time:xx

Ingredients:

- 1/2 cup mayonnaise
- 2 tsp sriracha sauce
- 1 jar dill pickle slices
- 1 egg
- 2 tbsp milk
- 50g flour
- 50g cornmeal
- ½ tsp seasoned salt
- ¼ tsp paprika
- ¼ tsp garlic powder
- ⅛ tsp pepper
- Cooking spray

Directions:

1. Mix the mayo and sriracha together in a bowl and set aside
2. Heat the air fryer to 200ºC
3. Drain the pickles and pat dry
4. Mix egg and milk together, in another bowl mix all the remaining ingredients
5. Dip the pickles in the egg mix then in the flour mix
6. Spray the air fryer with cooking spray
7. Cook for about 4 minutes until crispy

Asian Devilled Eggs

Servings: 12
Cooking Time:xx

Ingredients:

- 6 large eggs
- 2 tbsp mayo
- 1 ½ tsp sriracha
- 1 ½ tsp sesame oil
- 1 tsp soy sauce
- 1 tsp dijon mustard
- 1 tsp finely grated ginger
- 1 tsp rice vinegar
- 1 chopped green onion
- Toasted sesame seeds

Directions:

1. Set air fryer to 125ºC
2. Place eggs in the air fryer and cook for 15 minutes
3. Remove from the air fryer and place in a bowl of iced water for 10 minutes
4. Peel and cut in half
5. Scoop out the yolks and place in a food processor
6. Add the ingredients apart from the sesame seeds and green onion and combine until smooth
7. Place in a piping bag and pipe back into the egg whites
8. Garnish with seeds and green onion

Korean Chicken Wings

Servings: 2
Cooking Time:xx

Ingredients:

- 25ml soy sauce
- 40g brown sugar
- 2 tbsp hot pepper paste
- 1 tsp sesame oil
- ½ tsp ginger paste
- ½ tsp garlic paste
- 2 green onions, chopped
- 400g chicken wings
- 1 tbsp vegetable oil

Directions:

1. Preheat air fryer to 200ºC
2. Place all ingredients apart from chicken wings and vegetable oil in a pan and simmer for about 4 minutes set aside
3. Massage the vegetable oil into the chicken wings
4. Place in the air fryer and cook for about 10 minutes
5. Turn and cook for a further 10 minutes
6. Coat the wings in the sauce and return to the air fryer
7. Cook for about 2 minutes

Mini Calzones

Servings: 16
Cooking Time:xx

Ingredients:

- Flour for rolling out the dough
- 1 round pizza dough
- 100g pizza sauce

Directions:

1. Roll out the dough to ¼ inch thick
2. Cut out 8-10 dough rounds using a cutter
3. Re-roll the dough and cut out another 6 rounds
4. Top each round with pizza sauce, cheese and pepperoni
5. Fold dough over and pinch the edges to seal
6. Heat the air fryer to 190ºC
7. Place the calzone in the air fryer and cook for about 8 minutes until golden brown

Pao De Queijo

Servings: 20
Cooking Time:xx

Ingredients:

- 150g sweet starch
- 150g sour starch
- 50ml milk
- 25ml water
- 25ml olive oil
- 1 tsp salt
- 2 eggs
- 100g grated cheese
- 50g grated parmesan

Directions:

1. Preheat the air fryer to 170ºC
2. Mix the starch together in a bowl until well mixed
3. Add olive oil, milk and water to a pan, bring to the boil and reduce the heat
4. Add the starch and mix until all the liquid is absorbed
5. Add the eggs and mix to a dough
6. Add the cheeses and mix well
7. Form the dough into balls
8. Line the air fryer with parchment paper
9. Bake in the air fryer for 8-10 minutes

Beetroot Crisps

Servings: 2
Cooking Time:xx

Ingredients:

- 3 medium beetroots
- 2 tbsp oil
- Salt to taste

Directions:

1. Peel and thinly slice the beetroot
2. Coat with the oil and season with salt
3. Preheat the air fryer to 200ºC
4. Place in the air fryer and cook for 12-18 minutes until crispy

Chicken & Bacon Parcels

Servings: 4
Cooking Time:xx

Ingredients:

- 2 chicken breasts, boneless and skinless
- 200ml BBQ sauce
- 7 slices of bacon, cut lengthwise into halves
- 2 tbsp brown sugar

Directions:

1. Preheat the air fryer to 220ºC
2. Cut the chicken into strips, you should have 7 in total
3. Wrap two strips of the bacon around each piece of chicken
4. Brush the BBQ sauce over the top and sprinkle with the brown sugar
5. Place the chicken into the basket and cook for 5 minutes
6. Turn the chicken over and cook for another 5 minutes

Scotch Eggs

Servings: 6
Cooking Time:xx

Ingredients:

- 300g pork sausage
- 6 hard boiled eggs, shelled
- 50g cup flour
- 2 eggs, beaten
- 1 cup breadcrumbs
- Cooking spray

Directions:

1. Divide sausage into 6 portions
2. Place an egg in the middle of each portion and wrap around the egg
3. Dip the sausage in flour, then egg and then coat in breadcrumbs
4. Place in the air fryer and cook at 200°C for 12 minutes

Focaccia Bread

Servings: 8
Cooking Time:xx

Ingredients:

- 500g pizza dough
- 3 tbsp olive oil
- 2-3 garlic cloves, chopped
- ¼ tsp red pepper flakes
- 50g parsley
- 1 tsp basil
- 100g chopped red peppers
- 60g black olives halved
- 60g green olives halved
- Salt and pepper to taste

Directions:

1. Preheat the air fryer to 180°C, make indentations in the pizza dough with your finger tips and set aside
2. Heat the olive oil in a pan add the garlic and cook for a few minutes, add the remaining ingredients and cook for another 5-8 minutes not letting the oil get too hot
3. Spread the oil mix over the dough with a spatula
4. Place in the air fryer and cook for 12-15 minutes

Pretzel Bites

Servings: 2
Cooking Time:xx

Ingredients:

- 650g flour
- 2.5 tsp active dry yeast
- 260ml hot water
- 1 tsp salt
- 4 tbsp melted butter
- 2 tbsp sugar

Directions:

1. Take a large bowl and add the flour, sugar and salt
2. Take another bowl and combine the hot water and yeast, stirring until the yeast has dissolved
3. Then, add the yeast mixture to the flour mixture and use your hands to combine
4. Knead for 2 minutes
5. Cover the bowl with a kitchen towel for around half an hour
6. Divide the dough into 6 pieces
7. Preheat the air fryer to 260ºC
8. Take each section of dough and tear off a piece, rolling it in your hands to create a rope shape, that is around 1" in thickness
9. Cut into 2" strips
10. Place the small dough balls into the air fryer and leave a little space in-between
11. Cook for 6 minutes
12. Once cooked, remove and brush with melted butter and sprinkle salt on top

Jalapeño Pockets

Servings: 4
Cooking Time:xx

Ingredients:

- 1 chopped onion
- 60g cream cheese
- 1 jalapeño, chopped
- 8 wonton wrappers
- ¼ tsp garlic powder
- ⅛ tsp onion powder

Directions:

1. Cook the onion in a pan for 5 minutes until softened
2. Add to a bowl and mix with the remaining ingredients
3. Lay the wonton wrappers out and add filling to each one
4. Fold over to create a triangle and seal with water around the edges
5. Heat the air fryer to 200ºC
6. Place in the air fryer and cook for about 4 minutes

Jalapeño Poppers

Servings: 2
Cooking Time:xx

Ingredients:

- 10 jalapeños, halved and deseeded
- 100g cream cheese
- 50g parsley
- 150g breadcrumbs

Directions:

1. Mix 1/2 the breadcrumbs with the cream cheese
2. Add the parsley
3. Stuff the peppers with the cream cheese mix
4. Top the peppers with the remaining breadcrumbs
5. Heat the air fryer to 185ºC
6. Place in the air fryer and cook for 6-8 minutes

Bacon Smokies

Servings: 8
Cooking Time:xx
Ingredients:

- 150g little smokies (pieces)
- 150g bacon
- 50g brown sugar
- Toothpicks

Directions:

1. Cut the bacon strips into thirds
2. Put the brown sugar into a bowl
3. Coat the bacon with the sugar
4. Wrap the bacon around the little smokies and secure with a toothpick
5. Heat the air fryer to 170ºC
6. Place in the air fryer and cook for 10 minutes until crispy

Thai Bites

Servings: 4
Cooking Time:xx
Ingredients:

- 400g pork mince
- 1 onion
- 1 tsp garlic paste
- 1 tbsp soy
- 1 tbsp Worcester sauce
- Salt and pepper
- 2 tsp Thai curry paste
- ½ lime juice and zest
- 1 tsp mixed spice
- 1 tsp Chinese spice
- 1 tsp coriander

Directions:

1. Place all ingredients in a bowl and mix well
2. Shape into balls
3. Place in the air fryer and cook at 180ºC for 15 minutes

Waffle Fries

Servings: 4
Cooking Time:xx
Ingredients:

- 2 large potatoes, russet potatoes work best
- 1 tsp salt for seasoning
- Waffle cutter

Directions:

1. Peel the potatoes and slice using the waffle cutter. You can also use a mandolin cutter that has a blade
2. Transfer the potatoes to a bowl and season with the salt, coating evenly
3. Add to the air fryer and cook at 220ºC for 15 minutes, shaking every so often

Pasta Chips

Servings: 2
Cooking Time:xx

Ingredients:

- 300g dry pasta bows
- 1 tbsp olive oil
- 1 tbsp nutritional yeast
- 1½ tsp Italian seasoning
- ½ tsp salt

Directions:

1. Cook the pasta for half the time stated on the packet
2. Drain and mix with the oil, yeast, seasoning and salt
3. Place in the air fryer and cook at 200ºC for 5 minutes shake and cook for a further 3 minutes until crunchy

Onion Bahji

Servings: 8
Cooking Time:xx

Ingredients:

- 1 sliced red onion
- 1 sliced onion
- 1 tsp salt
- 1 minced jalapeño pepper
- 150g chickpea flour
- 4 tbsp water
- 1 clove garlic, minced
- 1 tsp coriander
- 1 tsp chilli powder
- 1 tsp turmeric
- ½ tsp cumin

Directions:

1. Place all ingredients in a bowl and mix well, leave to rest for 10 minutes
2. Preheat air fryer to 175ºC
3. Spray air fryer with cooking spray.
4. Form mix into bahji shapes and add to air fryer
5. Cook for 6 minutes turn and cook for a further 6 minutes

Spicy Chickpeas

Servings: 4
Cooking Time:xx

Ingredients:

- 1 can chickpeas
- 1 tbsp yeast
- 1 tbsp olive oil
- 1 tsp paprika
- 1 tsp garlic powder
- ½ tsp salt
- Pinch cumin

Directions:

1. Preheat air fryer to 180ºC
2. Combine all ingredients
3. Add to the air fryer and cook for 22 minutes tossing every 4 minutes until cooked

Beef & Lamb And Pork Recipes

Cheesy Meatballs

Servings: 2
Cooking Time:xx

Ingredients:

- 500g ground beef
- 1 can of chopped green chillis
- 1 egg white
- 1 tbsp water
- 2 tbsp taco seasoning
- 16 pieces of pepper jack cheese, cut into cubes
- 300g nacho cheese tortilla chips, crushed
- 6 tbsp taco sauce
- 3 tbsp honey

Directions:

1. Take a large bowl and combine the beef with the green collie sand taco seasoning
2. Use your hands to create meatballs - you should get around 15 balls in total
3. Place a cube of cheese in the middle of each meatball, forming the ball around it once more
4. Take a small bowl and beat the egg white
5. Take a large bowl and add the crushed chips
6. Dip every meatball into the egg white and then the crushed chips
7. Place the balls into the air fryer and cook at 260ºC for 14 minutes, turning halfway
8. Take a microwave-safe bowl and combine the honey and taco sauce
9. Place in the microwave for 30 seconds and serve the sauce warm with the meatballs

Beef Stroganoff

Servings:4
Cooking Time:20 Minutes

Ingredients:

- 4 cubes / 800 ml beef stock cubes
- 4 tbsp olive oil
- 1 onion, chopped
- 200 g / 7 oz sour cream
- 200 g / 7 oz mushroom, finely sliced
- 500 g / 17.6 oz steak, chopped
- 4 x 100 g / 3.5 oz egg noodles, cooked

Directions:

1. Preheat the air fryer to 200 °C / 400 °F and line the bottom of the basket with parchment paper.
2. Boil 800 ml of water and use it to dissolve the 4 beef stock cubes.
3. In a heat-proof bowl, mix the olive oil, onion, sour cream, mushrooms, and beef stock until fully combined.
4. Coat all sides of the steak chunks in the mixture and set aside to marinate for 10 minutes.
5. Transfer the steak to the air fryer, close the lid, and cook for 10 minutes. Serve the steak hot with a serving of egg noodles.

Asian Meatballs

Servings: 2
Cooking Time:xx

Ingredients:

- 500g minced pork
- 2 eggs
- 100g breadcrumbs
- 1 tsp minced garlic
- ⅓ tsp chilli flakes
- 1 tsp minced ginger
- 1 tsp sesame oil
- 1 tsp soy
- 2 diced spring onions
- Salt and pepper to taste

Directions:

1. Mix all ingredients in a bowl until combined
2. Form mix into 1 ½ inch meatballs
3. Place in the air fryer and cook at 200ºC for about 10 minutes until cooked

Lamb Calzone

Servings: 2
Cooking Time:xx

Ingredients:

- 1 tsp olive oil
- 1 chopped onion
- 100g baby spinach leaves
- 400g minced pork
- 250g whole wheat pizza dough
- 300g grated cheese

Directions:

1. Heat the olive oil in a pan, add the onion and cook for about 2 minutes
2. Add the spinach and cook for a further 1 ½ minutes
3. Stir in marinara sauce and the minced pork
4. Divide the dough into four and roll out into circles
5. Add ¼ of filling to each piece of dough
6. Sprinkle with cheese and fold the dough over to create half moons, crimp edges to seal
7. Spray with cooking spray, place in the air fryer and cook at 160ºC for 12 minutes turning after 8 minutes

Southern Style Pork Chops

Servings: 4
Cooking Time:xx

Ingredients:

- 4 pork chops
- 3 tbsp buttermilk
- 100g flour
- Salt and pepper to taste
- Pork rub to taste

Directions:

1. Season the pork with pork rub
2. Drizzle with buttermilk
3. Coat in flour until fully covered
4. Place the pork chops in the air fryer, cook at 170ºC for 15 minutes
5. Turnover and cook for a further 10 minutes

Pork Belly With Crackling

Servings: 4
Cooking Time:xx

Ingredients:

- 800g belly pork
- 1 tsp sea salt
- 1 tsp garlic salt
- 2 tsp five spice
- 1 tsp rosemary
- 1 tsp white pepper
- 1 tsp sugar
- Half a lemon

Directions:

1. Cut lines into the meat portion of the belly pork
2. Cook thoroughly in water
3. Allow to air dry for 3 hours
4. Score the skin and prick holes with a fork
5. Rub with the dry rub mix, rub some lemon juice on the skin
6. Place in the air fryer and cook at 160ºC for 30 minutes then at 180ºC for a further 30 minutes

Cheese & Ham Sliders

Servings: 4
Cooking Time:xx

Ingredients:

- 8 slider bread rolls, cut in half
- 16 slices of sweet ham
- 16 slices of Swiss cheese
- 5 tbsp mayonnaise
- 1/2 tsp paprika
- 1 tsp onion powder
- 1 tsp dill

Directions:

1. Place 2 slices of ham into each bread roll and 2 slices of cheese
2. Take a bowl and combine the mayonnaise with the onion powder, dill and paprika
3. Add half a tablespoon of the sauce on top of each piece of cheese
4. Place the top on the bread slider
5. Cook at 220ºC for 5 minutes

Air Fryer Pork Bratwurst

Servings: 2
Cooking Time:xx

Ingredients:

- 2 pork bratwursts
- 2 hotdog bread rolls
- 2 tbsp tomato sauce

Directions:

1. Preheat the air fryer to 200ºC
2. Place the bratwurst in the fryer and cook for 10 minutes, turning halfway
3. Remove and place in the open bread rolls
4. Place back into the air fryer for 1 to 2 minutes, until the read is slightly crisped
5. Enjoy with the tomato sauce either on top or on the side

Steak Popcorn Bites

Servings: 4
Cooking Time:xx

Ingredients:

- 500g steak, cut into 1" sized cubes
- 500g potato chips, ridged ones work best
- 100g flour
- 2 beaten eggs
- Salt and pepper to taste

Directions:

1. Place the chips into the food processor and pulse unit you get fine chip crumbs
2. Take a bowl and combine the flour with salt and pepper
3. Add the chips to another bowl and the beaten egg to another bowl
4. Take the steak cubes and dip first in the flour, then the egg and then the chip crumbs
5. Preheat your air fryer to 260ºC
6. Place the steak pieces into the fryer and cook for 9 minutes

Roast Pork

Servings: 4
Cooking Time:xx

Ingredients:

- 500g pork joint
- 1 tbsp olive oil
- 1 tsp salt

Directions:

1. Preheat air fryer to 180ºC
2. Score the pork skin with a knife
3. Drizzle the pork with oil and rub it into the skin, sprinkle with salt
4. Place in the air fryer and cook for about 50 minutes

Beef Wellington

Servings: 4
Cooking Time:xx

Ingredients:

- 300g chicken liver pate
- 500g shortcrust pastry
- 600g beef fillet
- 1 egg beaten
- Salt and pepper

Directions:

1. Remove all the visible fat from the beef season with salt and pepper. Wrap in cling film and place in the fridge for 1 hour
2. Roll out the pastry, brush the edges with egg
3. Spread the pate over the pastry. Remove the clingfilm from the beef and place in the center of the pastry
4. Seal the pastry around the meat
5. Place in the air fryer and cook at 160ºC for 35 minutes

Italian Meatballs

Servings: 12
Cooking Time:xx

Ingredients:

- 2 tbsp olive oil
- 2 tbsp minced shallot
- 3 cloves garlic minced
- 100g panko crumbs
- 35g chopped parsley
- 1 tbsp chopped rosemary
- 60ml milk
- 400g minced pork
- 250g turkey sausage
- 1 egg beaten
- 1 tbsp dijon mustard
- 1 tbsp finely chopped thyme

Directions:

1. Preheat air fryer to 200ºC
2. Heat oil in a pan and cook the garlic and shallot over a medium heat for 1-2 minutes
3. Mix the panko and milk in a bowl and allow to stand for 5 minutes
4. Add all the ingredients to the panko mix and combine well
5. Shape into 1 ½ inch meatballs and cook for 12 minutes

Lamb Burgers

Servings: 4
Cooking Time:xx

Ingredients:

- 600g minced lamb
- 2 tsp garlic puree
- 1 tsp harissa paste
- 2 tbsp Moroccan spice
- Salt and pepper

Directions:

1. Place all the ingredients in a bowl and mix well
2. Form into patties
3. Place in the air fryer and cook at 180ºC for 18 minutes

Mustard Pork Tenderloin

Servings: 2
Cooking Time:xx

Ingredients:

- 1 pork tenderloin
- 3 tbsp soy sauce
- 2 minced garlic cloves
- 3 tbsp olive oil
- 2 tbsp brown sugar
- 1 tbsp dijon mustard
- Salt and pepper for seasoning

Directions:

1. Take a bowl and combine the ingredients, except for the pork
2. Pour the mixture into a ziplock bag and then add the pork
3. Close the top and make sure the pork is well covered
4. Place in the refrigerator for 30minutes
5. Preheat your air fryer to 260ºC
6. Remove the pork from the bag and place in the fryer
7. Cook for 25 minutes, turning halfway
8. Remove and rest for 5 minutes before slicing into pieces

Pulled Pork, Bacon, And Cheese Sliders

Servings:2
Cooking Time:30 Minutes

Ingredients:

- 2 x 50 g / 3.5 oz pork steaks
- 1 tsp salt
- 1 tsp black pepper
- 4 slices bacon strips, chopped into small pieces
- 1 tbsp soy sauce
- 1 tbsp BBQ sauce
- 100 g / 7 oz cheddar cheese, grated
- 2 bread buns

Directions:

1. Preheat the air fryer to 200 °C / 400 °F and line the bottom of the basket with parchment paper.
2. Place the pork steaks on a clean surface and season with salt and black pepper. Move the pork steak in the prepared air fryer basket and cook for 15 minutes.
3. Remove the steak from the air fryer and shred using two forks. Mix with the chopped bacon in a heatproof bowl and place the bowl in the air fryer. Cook for 10 minutes.
4. Remove the bowl from the air fryer and stir in the soy sauce and BBQ sauce. Return the bowl to the air fryer basket and continue cooking for a further 5 minutes.
5. Meanwhile, spread the cheese across one half of the bread buns. Top with the cooked pulled pork and an extra squirt of BBQ sauce.

Breaded Pork Chops

Servings: 6
Cooking Time:xx

Ingredients:

- 6 boneless pork chops
- 1 beaten egg
- 100g panko crumbs
- 75g crushed cornflakes
- 2 tbsp parmesan
- 1 ¼ tsp paprika
- ½ tsp garlic powder
- ½ tsp onion powder
- ¼ tsp chilli powder
- Salt and pepper to taste

Directions:

1. Heat the air fryer to 200ºC
2. Season the pork chops with salt
3. Mix the panko, cornflakes, salt, parmesan, garlic powder, onion powder, paprika, chilli powder and pepper in a bowl
4. Beat the egg in another bowl
5. Dip the pork in the egg and then coat with panko mix
6. Place in the air fryer and cook for about 12 minutes turning halfway

Steak Fajitas

Servings: 4
Cooking Time:xx
Ingredients:

- 500g sliced steak
- 25g pineapple juice
- 2 tbsp lime juice
- 1 tbsp olive oil
- 1 tbsp soy sauce
- 1 tbsp minced garlic
- ½ tbsp chilli powder
- 1/2 tsp paprika
- 1 tsp cumin
- 1 pepper
- 1 onion
- Salt and pepper to taste

Directions:

1. Mix pineapple juice, lime juice, olive oil, soy sauce, garlic, cumin chilli powder and paprika. Pour over the steak and marinate for 4 hours
2. Line the air fryer with foil, add the peppers and onions, season with salt and pepper
3. Cook at 200ºC for 10 minutes, add the steak and cook for another 7 minutes
4. Serve with tortillas
5. Set your fryer to 170ºC and cook the sandwich for 4 minutes
6. Turn the sandwich over and cook for another 3 minutes
7. Turn the sandwich out and serve whilst hot
8. Repeat with the other remaining sandwich

Mustard Glazed Pork

Servings: 4
Cooking Time:xx
Ingredients:

- 500g pork tenderloin
- 1 tbsp minced garlic
- ¼ tsp salt
- ⅛ tsp cracked black pepper
- 75g yellow mustard
- 3 tbsp brown sugar
- 1 tsp Italian seasoning
- 1 tsp rosemary

Directions:

1. Cut slits into the pork place the minced garlic into the slits, season with the salt and pepper
2. Add the remaining ingredients to a bowl and whisk to combine
3. Rub the mix over the pork and allow to marinate for 2 hours
4. Place in the air fryer and cook at 200ºC for 20 minutes

Beef And Cheese Empanadas

Servings: 12
Cooking Time:xx

Ingredients:

- 2 tsp oil
- 1 chopped onion
- 1 clove chopped garlic
- 500g minced beef
- Salt and pepper
- 2 tbsp chopped jalapeño
- 2 packs ready made pastry
- 50g grated cheddar cheese
- 50g pepper jack cheese
- 1 egg

Directions:

1. Heat the oil in a pan and fry the onion and garlic until soft
2. Add the meat and jalapeño, season with salt and pepper, and cook until browned
3. Allow the meat to cool
4. Roll out dough as thin as possible and cut into circles, fill with 1 tablespoon of mix, sprinkle with cheese, fold over and seal with the egg
5. Set your fryer to 170ºC and cook for about 12 minutes until golden brown

Pork With Chinese 5 Spice

Servings: 4
Cooking Time:xx

Ingredients:

- 2 pork rounds cut into chunks
- 2 large eggs
- 1 tsp sesame oil
- 200g cornstarch
- 1/4 tsp salt
- ½ tsp pepper
- 3 tbsp canola oil
- 1 tsp Chinese 5 spice

Directions:

1. In a bowl mix the corn starch, salt, pepper and 5 spice
2. Mix the eggs and sesame oil in another bowl
3. Dip the pork into the egg and then cover in the corn starch mix
4. Place in the air fryer and cook at 170ºC for 11-12 minutes, shaking halfway through
5. Serve with sweet and sour sauce

Poultry Recipes

Thai Turkey Burgers

Servings: 4
Cooking Time:xx
Ingredients:

- 1 courgette/zucchini, about 200 g/7 oz.
- 400 g/14 oz. minced/ground turkey breast
- 35 g/½ cup fresh breadcrumbs (gluten-free if you wish)
- 1 teaspoon Thai 7 spice seasoning
- 1 teaspoon salt
- 1 teaspoon olive oil

Directions:

1. Coarsely grate the courgette/zucchini, then place in a piece of muslin/cheesecloth and squeeze out the water. Combine the grated courgette with all other ingredients except the olive oil, mixing together well. Divide the mixture into 4 equal portions and mould into burgers. Brush with oil.
2. Preheat the air-fryer to 190°C/375°C.
3. Add the turkey burgers to the preheated air-fryer and air-fry for 15 minutes, turning once halfway through cooking. Check the internal temperature of the burgers has reached at least 74°C/165°F using a meat thermometer – if not, cook for another few minutes and then serve.

Bbq Chicken Tenders

Servings: 6
Cooking Time:xx
Ingredients:

- 300g barbecue flavoured pork rinds
- 200g all purpose flour
- 1 tbsp barbecue seasoning
- 1 egg
- 400g chicken breast tenderloins
- Cooking spray

Directions:

1. Preheat the air fryer to 190°C
2. Place the pork rinds into a food processor and blitz to a breadcrumb consistency, before transferring to a bowl
3. In a separate bowl, combine the flour and barbecue seasoning
4. Beat the egg in a small bowl
5. Take the chicken and first dip into the egg, then the flour, and then the breadcrumbs
6. Place the chicken into the air fryer and spray with cooking spray and cook for about 15 minutes

Crunchy Chicken Tenders

Servings: 4
Cooking Time:xx

Ingredients:

- 8 regular chicken tenders (frozen work best)
- 1 egg
- 2 tbsp olive oil
- 150g dried breadcrumbs

Directions:

1. Heat the fryer to 175ºC
2. In a small bowl, beat the egg
3. In another bowl, combine the oil and the breadcrumbs together
4. Take one tender and first dip it into the egg, and then cover it in the breadcrumb mixture
5. Place the tender into the fryer basket
6. Repeat with the rest of the tenders, arranging them carefully so they don't touch inside the basket
7. Cook for 12 minutes, checking that they are white in the centre before serving

Air Fried Maple Chicken Thighs

Servings: 4
Cooking Time:xx

Ingredients:

- 200ml buttermilk
- ½ tbsp maple syrup
- 1 egg
- 1 tsp granulated garlic salt
- 4 chicken thighs with the bone in
- 140g all purpose flour
- 65g tapioca flour
- 1 tsp sweet paprika
- 1 tsp onion powder
- ¼ tsp ground black pepper
- ¼ tsp cayenne pepper
- ½ tsp granulated garlic
- ½ tsp honey powder

Directions:

1. Take a bowl and combine the buttermilk, maple syrup, egg and garlic powder
2. Transfer to a bag and add chicken thighs, shaking to combine well
3. Set aside for 1 hour
4. Take a shallow bowl and add the flour, tapioca flour, salt, sweet paprika, smoked paprika, pepper, cayenne pepper and honey powder, combining well
5. Preheat the air fryer to 190ºC
6. Drag the chicken through flour mixture and place the chicken skin side down in the air fryer Cook for 12 minutes, until white in the middle

Garlic Parmesan Fried Chicken Wings

Servings: 4
Cooking Time:xx

Ingredients:

- 16 chicken wing drumettes
- Cooking spray
- 240ml low fat buttermilk
- 150g flour
- 140g grated parmesan
- 2 tbsp low sodium soy sauce
- 1 sachet of your favourite chicken seasoning
- 1 tsp garlic powder
- Salt and pepper to taste

Directions:

1. Place the chicken onto a cooking tray and pour the soy sauce over the top, ensuring it is fully coated
2. Season the chicken and place in the refrigerator for 30 minutes
3. Add the flour and parmesan into a ziplock bag
4. Coat the chicken with buttermilk and add it to the ziplock bag with the flour
5. Preheat your air fryer to 200ºC
6. Place the chicken into the air fryer for 20 minutes
7. Shake the air fryer basket every 5 minutes until the 20 minutes is up

Chicken Tikka

Servings: 2
Cooking Time:xx

Ingredients:

- 2 chicken breasts, diced
- FIRST MARINADE
- freshly squeezed juice of ½ a lemon
- 1 tablespoon freshly grated ginger
- 1 tablespoon freshly grated garlic
- a good pinch of salt
- SECOND MARINADE
- 100 g/½ cup Greek yogurt
- ½ teaspoon chilli powder
- ½ teaspoon chilli paste
- ½ teaspoon turmeric
- ½ teaspoon garam masala
- 1 tablespoon olive oil

Directions:

1. Mix the ingredients for the first marinade together in a bowl, add in the chicken and stir to coat all the chicken pieces. Leave in the fridge to marinate for 20 minutes.
2. Combine the second marinade ingredients. Once the first marinade has had 20 minutes, add the second marinade to the chicken and stir well. Leave in the fridge for at least 4 hours.
3. Preheat the air-fryer to 180ºC/350ºF.
4. Thread the chicken pieces onto metal skewers that fit in your air-fryer. Add the skewers to the preheated air-fryer and air-fry for 10 minutes. Check the internal temperature of the chicken has reached at least 74ºC/165ºF using a meat thermometer – if not, cook for another few minutes and then serve.

Air Fryer Sesame Chicken Thighs

Servings: 4
Cooking Time:xx

Ingredients:

- 2 tbsp sesame oil
- 2 tbsp soy sauce
- 1 tbsp honey
- 1 tbsp sriracha sauce
- 1 tsp rice vinegar
- 400g chicken thighs
- 1 green onion, chopped
- 2 tbsp toasted sesame seeds

Directions:

1. Take a large bowl and combine the sesame oil, soy sauce, honey, sriracha and vinegar
2. Add the chicken and refrigerate for 30 minutes
3. Preheat the air fryer to 200ºC
4. Cook for 5 minutes
5. Flip and then cook for another 10 minutes
6. Serve with green onion and sesame seeds

Cornflake Chicken Nuggets

Servings: 4
Cooking Time:xx

Ingredients:

- 100 g/4 cups cornflakes (gluten-free if you wish)
- 70 g/½ cup plus ½ tablespoon plain/all-purpose flour (gluten-free if you wish)
- 2 eggs, beaten
- ½ teaspoon salt
- ¼ teaspoon freshly ground black pepper
- 600 g/1 lb. 5 oz. mini chicken fillets

Directions:

1. Grind the cornflakes in a food processor to a crumb-like texture. Place the flour in one bowl and the beaten eggs in a second bowl; season both bowls with the salt and pepper. Coat each chicken fillet in flour, tapping off any excess. Next dip each flour-coated chicken fillet into the egg, then the cornflakes until fully coated.
2. Preheat the air-fryer to 180ºC/350ºF.
3. Add the chicken fillets to the preheated air-fryer (you may need to add the fillets in two batches, depending on the size of your air-fryer) and air-fry for 10 minutes, turning halfway through cooking. Check the internal temperature of the nuggets has reached at least 74ºC/165ºF using a meat thermometer – if not, cook for another few minutes and then serve.
4. VARIATION: SIMPLE CHICKEN NUGGETS
5. For a simpler version, replace the crushed cornflakes with 90 g/1¼ cups dried breadcrumbs (see page 9). Prepare and air-fry in the same way.

Chicken Milanese

Servings: 4
Cooking Time:xx

Ingredients:

- 130 g/1¾ cups dried breadcrumbs (gluten-free if you wish, see page 9)
- 50 g/⅔ cup grated Parmesan
- 1 teaspoon dried basil
- ½ teaspoon dried thyme
- ¼ teaspoon freshly ground black pepper
- 1 egg, beaten
- 4 tablespoons plain/all-purpose flour (gluten-free if you wish)
- 4 boneless chicken breasts

Directions:

1. Combine the breadcrumbs, cheese, herbs and pepper in a bowl. In a second bowl beat the egg, and in the third bowl have the plain/all-purpose flour. Dip each chicken breast first into the flour, then the egg, then the seasoned breadcrumbs.
2. Preheat the air-fryer to 180°C/350°F.
3. Add the breaded chicken breasts to the preheated air-fryer and air-fry for 12 minutes. Check the internal temperature of the chicken has reached at least 74°C/165°F using a meat thermometer – if not, cook for another few minutes.

Turkey Cutlets In Mushroom Sauce

Servings: 2
Cooking Time:xx

Ingredients:

- 2 turkey cutlets
- 1 tbsp butter
- 1 can of cream of mushroom sauce
- 160ml milk
- Salt and pepper for seasoning

Directions:

1. Preheat the air fryer to 220°C
2. Brush the turkey cults with the butter and seasoning
3. Place in the air fryer and cook for 11 minutes
4. Add the mushroom soup and milk to a pan and cook over the stone for around 10 minutes, stirring every so often
5. Top the turkey cutlets with the sauce

Pizza Chicken Nuggets

Servings: 2
Cooking Time:xx

Ingredients:

- 60 g/¾ cup dried breadcrumbs (see page 9)
- 20 g/¼ cup grated Parmesan
- ½ teaspoon dried oregano
- ¼ teaspoon freshly ground black pepper
- 150 g/⅔ cup Mediterranean sauce (see page 102) or 150 g/5½ oz. jarred tomato pasta sauce (keep any leftover sauce for serving)
- 400 g/14 oz. chicken fillets

Directions:

1. Preheat the air-fryer to 180°C/350°F.
2. Combine the breadcrumbs, Parmesan, oregano and pepper in a bowl. Have the Mediterranean or pasta sauce in a separate bowl.
3. Dip each chicken fillet in the tomato sauce first, then roll in the breadcrumb mix until coated fully.
4. Add the breaded fillets to the preheated air-fryer and air-fry for 10 minutes. Check the internal temperature of the chicken has reached at least 74°C/165°F using a meat thermometer – if not, cook for another few minutes.
5. Serve with some additional sauce that has been warmed through.

Chicken Fajitas

Servings: 3
Cooking Time:xx

Ingredients:

- 2 boneless chicken breasts, sliced into strips
- 5 mini (bell) peppers, sliced into strips
- 1 courgette/zucchini, sliced into 5-mm/¼-in. thick discs
- 2 tablespoons olive oil
- 28-g/1-oz. packet fajita seasoning mix
- TO SERVE
- wraps
- sliced avocado
- chopped tomato and red onion
- grated Red Leicester cheese
- plain yogurt
- coriander/cilantro
- lime wedges, for squeezing

Directions:

1. Combine the chicken, (bell) peppers, courgettes/zucchini and olive oil in a bowl. Add the fajita seasoning and stir to coat.
2. Preheat the air-fryer to 180ºC/350ºF.
3. Add the coated vegetables and chicken to the preheated air-fryer and air-fry for 12 minutes, shaking the drawer a couple of times during cooking. Check the internal temperature of the chicken has reached at least 74ºC/165ºF using a meat thermometer – if not, cook for another few minutes.
4. Serve immediately alongside the serving suggestions or your own choices of accompaniments.

Chicken Kiev

Servings: 4
Cooking Time:xx

Ingredients:

- 4 boneless chicken breasts
- 4 tablespoons plain/all-purpose flour (gluten-free if you wish)
- 1 egg, beaten
- 130 g/2 cups dried breadcrumbs (gluten-free if you wish, see page 9)
- GARLIC BUTTER
- 60 g/4 tablespoons salted butter, softened
- 1 large garlic clove, finely chopped

Directions:

1. Mash together the butter and garlic. Form into a sausage shape, then slice into 4 equal discs. Place in the freezer until frozen.
2. Make a deep horizontal slit across each chicken breast, taking care not to cut through to the other side. Stuff the cavity with a disc of frozen garlic butter. Place the flour in a shallow bowl, the egg in another and the breadcrumbs in a third. Coat each chicken breast first in flour, then egg, then breadcrumbs.
3. Preheat the air-fryer to 180ºC/350ºF.
4. Add the chicken Kievs to the preheated air-fryer and air-fry for 12 minutes until cooked through. This is hard to gauge as the butter inside the breast is not an indicator of doneness, so test the meat in the centre with a meat thermometer – it should be at least 75ºC/167ºF; if not, cook for another few minutes.

Chicken And Cheese Chimichangas

Servings: 6
Cooking Time:xx

Ingredients:

- 100g shredded chicken (cooked)
- 150g nacho cheese
- 1 chopped jalapeño pepper
- 6 flour tortillas
- 5 tbsp salsa
- 60g refried beans
- 1 tsp cumin
- 0.5 tsp chill powder
- Salt and pepper to taste

Directions:

1. Take a large mixing bowl and add all of the ingredients, combining well
2. Add ⅓ of the filling to each tortilla and roll into a burrito shape
3. Spray the air fryer with cooking spray and heat to 200ºC
4. Place the chimichangas in the air fryer and cook for 7 minutes

Spicy Chicken Wing Drummettes

Servings: 4
Cooking Time:xx

Ingredients:

- 10 large chicken drumettes
- Cooking spray
- 100ml rice vinegar
- 3 tbsp honey
- 2 tbsp unsalted chicken stock
- 1 tbsp lower sodium soy sauce
- 1 tbsp toasted sesame oil
- ⅜ tsp crushed red pepper
- 1 garlic clove, finely chopped
- 2 tbsp chopped, unsalted, roasted peanuts
- 1 tbsp chopped fresh chives

Directions:

1. Coat the chicken in cooking spray and place inside the air fryer
2. Cook at 200ºC for 30 minutes
3. Take a mixing bowl and combine the vinegar, honey, stock, soy sauce, oil, crushed red pepper and garlic
4. Cook to a simmer, until a syrup consistency is achieved
5. Coat the chicken in this mixture and sprinkle with peanuts and chives

Chicken & Potatoes

Servings: 4
Cooking Time:xx

Ingredients:

- 2 tbsp olive oil
- 2 potatoes, cut into 2" pieces
- 2 chicken breasts, cut into pieces of around 1" size
- 4 crushed garlic cloves
- 2 tsp smoked paprika
- 1 tsp thyme
- 1/2 tsp red chilli flakes
- Salt and pepper to taste

Directions:

1. Preheat your air fryer to 260ºC
2. Take a large bowl and combine the potatoes with half of the garlic, half the paprika, half the chilli flakes, salt, pepper and half the oil
3. Place into the air fryer and cook for 5 minutes, before turning over and cooking for another 5 minutes
4. Take a bowl and add the chicken with the rest of the seasonings and oil, until totally coated
5. Add the chicken to the potatoes mixture, moving the potatoes to the side
6. Cook for 10 minutes, turning the chicken halfway through

Sticky Chicken Tikka Drumsticks

Servings: 4
Cooking Time:xx

Ingredients:

- 12 chicken drumsticks
- MARINADE
- 100 g/½ cup Greek yogurt
- 2 tablespoons tikka paste
- 2 teaspoons ginger preserve
- freshly squeezed juice of ½ a lemon
- ¾ teaspoon salt

Directions:

1. Make slices across each of the drumsticks with a sharp knife. Mix the marinade ingredients together in a bowl, then add the drumsticks. Massage the marinade into the drumsticks, then leave to marinate in the fridge overnight or for at least 6 hours.
2. Preheat the air-fryer to 200ºC/400ºF.
3. Lay the drumsticks on an air-fryer liner or a piece of pierced parchment paper. Place the paper and drumsticks in the preheated air-fryer. Air-fry for 6 minutes, then turn over and cook for a further 6 minutes. Check the internal temperature of the drumsticks has reached at least 75ºC/167ºF using a meat thermometer – if not, cook for another few minutes and then serve.

Air Fryer Chicken Thigh Schnitzel

Servings: 4

Cooking Time:xx

Ingredients:

- 300g boneless chicken thighs
- 160g seasoned breadcrumbs
- 1 tsp salt
- ½ tsp ground black pepper
- 30g flour
- 1 egg
- Cooking spray

Directions:

1. Lay the chicken on a sheet of parchment paper and add another on top
2. Use a mallet or a rolling pin to flatten it down
3. Take a bowl and add the breadcrumbs with the salt and pepper
4. Place the flour into another bowl
5. Dip the chicken into the flour, then the egg, and then the breadcrumbs
6. Preheat air fryer to 190ºC
7. Place the chicken into the air fryer and spray with cooking oil
8. Cook for 6 minutes

Whole Chicken

Servings: 4

Cooking Time:xx

Ingredients:

- 1.5-kg/3¼-lb. chicken
- 2 tablespoons butter or coconut oil
- salt and freshly ground black pepper

Directions:

1. Place the chicken breast-side up and carefully insert the butter or oil between the skin and the flesh of each breast. Season.
2. Preheat the air-fryer to 180ºC/350ºF. If the chicken hits the heating element, remove the drawer to lower the chicken a level.
3. Add the chicken to the preheated air-fryer breast-side up. Air-fry for 30 minutes, then turn over and cook for a further 10 minutes. Check the internal temperature with a meat thermometer. If it is 75ºC/167ºF at the thickest part, remove the chicken from the air-fryer and leave to rest for 10 minutes before carving. If less than 75ºC/167ºF, continue to cook until this internal temperature is reached and then allow to rest.

Chicken Tikka Masala

Servings: 4
Cooking Time:xx

Ingredients:

- 100g tikka masala curry pasta
- 200g low fat yogurt
- 600g skinless chicken breasts
- 1 tbsp vegetable oil
- 1 onion, chopped
- 400g can of the whole, peeled tomatoes
- 20ml water
- 1 tbsp sugar
- 2 tbsp lemon juice
- 1 small bunch of chopped coriander leaves

Directions:

1. Take a bowl and combine the tikka masala curry paste with half the yogurt
2. Cut the chicken into strips
3. Preheat the air fryer to 200ºC
4. Add the yogurt mixture and coat the chicken until fully covered
5. Place into the refrigerator for 2 hours
6. Place the oil and onion in the air fryer and cook for 10 minutes
7. Add the marinated chicken, tomatoes, water and the rest of the yogurt and combine
8. Add the sugar and lemon juice and combine again
9. Cook for 15 minutes

Fish & Seafood Recipes

Oat & Parmesan Crusted Fish Fillets

Servings: 2
Cooking Time:xx
Ingredients:

- 20 g/⅓ cup fresh breadcrumbs
- 25 g/3 tablespoons oats
- 15 g/¼ cup grated Parmesan
- 1 egg
- 2 x 175-g/6-oz. white fish fillets, skin-on
- salt and freshly ground black pepper

Directions:

1. Preheat the air-fryer to 180ºC/350ºF.
2. Combine the breadcrumbs, oats and cheese in a bowl and stir in a pinch of salt and pepper. In another bowl beat the egg. Dip the fish fillets in the egg, then top with the oat mixture.
3. Add the fish fillets to the preheated air-fryer on an air-fryer liner or a piece of pierced parchment paper. Air-fry for 10 minutes. Check the fish is just flaking away when a fork is inserted, then serve immediately.

Lobster Tails

Servings: 2
Cooking Time:xx
Ingredients:

- 4 lobster tails
- 2 tbsp melted butter
- ½ tsp salt
- 1 tsp pepper

Directions:

1. Cut the lobster tails through the tail section and pull back the shell
2. Brush with the melted butter and sprinkle with salt and pepper
3. Heat the air fryer to 200ºC and cook for 4 minutes
4. Brush with melted butter and cook for a further 2 minutes

Traditional Fish And Chips

Servings: 4
Cooking Time:xx
Ingredients:

- 4 potatoes, peeled and cut into chips
- 2 fish fillets of your choice
- 1 beaten egg
- 3 slices of wholemeal bread, grated into breadcrumbs
- 25g tortilla crisps
- 1 lemon rind and juice
- 1 tbsp parsley
- Salt and pepper to taste

Directions:

1. Preheat your air fryer to 200ºC
2. Place the chips inside and cook until crispy
3. Cut the fish fillets into 4 slices and season with lemon juice
4. Place the breadcrumbs, lemon rind, parsley, tortillas and seasoning into a food processor and blitz to create a crumb consistency
5. Place the breadcrumbs on a large plate
6. Coat the fish in the egg and then the breadcrumb mixture
7. Cook for 15 minutes at 180ºC

Cod Nuggets

Servings: 4
Cooking Time:xx

Ingredients:

- 400g cod fillets, cut into 8 chunks
- 35g flour
- 1 tbsp vegetable oil
- 200g cornflakes or cracker crumbs
- Egg wash - 1 tbsp egg and 1 tbsp water
- Salt and pepper to taste

Directions:

1. Crush the crackers or cornflakes to make crumbs, mix in the vegetable oil
2. Season the cod with salt and pepper and cover in flour, dip into the egg-wash then cover in crumbs
3. Set the air fryer to 180°C
4. Place the cod nuggets in the air fryer basket and cook for 15 minutes, until golden brown.

Ranch Style Fish Fillets

Servings: 4
Cooking Time:xx

Ingredients:

- 200g bread crumbs
- 30g ranch-style dressing mix
- 2 tbsp oil
- 2 beaten eggs
- 4 fish fillets of your choice
- Lemon wedges to garnish

Directions:

1. Preheat air fryer to 180°C
2. Mix the bread crumbs and ranch dressing mix together, add in the oil until the mix becomes crumbly
3. Dip the fish into the, then cover in the breadcrumb mix
4. Place in the air fryer and cook for 12-13 minutes

Thai Fish Cakes

Servings: 4
Cooking Time:xx

Ingredients:

- 200g pre-mashed potatoes
- 2 fillets of white fish, flaked and mashed
- 1 onion
- 1 tsp butter
- 1 tsp milk
- 1 lime zest and rind
- 3 tsp chilli
- 1 tsp Worcester sauce
- 1 tsp coriander
- 1 tsp mixed spice
- 1 tsp mixed herbs
- 50g breadcrumbs
- Salt and pepper to taste

Directions:

1. Cover the white fish in milk
2. in a mixing bowl place the fish and add the seasoning and mashed potatoes
3. Add the butter and remaining milk
4. Use your hands to create patties and place in the refrigerator for 3 hours
5. Preheat your air fryer to 200°C
6. Cook for 15 minutes

Furikake Salmon

Servings: 2
Cooking Time:xx

Ingredients:

- 1 salmon fillet
- 2 tbsp furikake
- 150ml mayonnaise
- 1 tbsp shoe
- Salt and pepper for seasoning

Directions:

1. Preheat the air fryer to 230ºC
2. Take a small bowl and combine the mayonnaise and shoyu
3. Add salt and pepper to the salmon on both sides
4. Place in the air fryer with the skin facing downwards
5. Brush a layer of the mayonnaise mixture on top of the salmon
6. Sprinkle the furikake on top
7. Cook for 10 minutes

Copycat Fish Fingers

Servings: 2
Cooking Time:xx

Ingredients:

- 2 slices wholemeal bread, grated into breadcrumbs
- 50g plain flour
- 1 beaten egg
- 1 white fish fillet
- The juice of 1 small lemon
- 1 tsp parsley
- 1 tsp thyme
- 1 tsp mixed herbs
- Salt and pepper to taste

Directions:

1. Preheat the air fryer to 180ºC
2. Add salt pepper and parsley to the breadcrumbs and combine well
3. Place the egg in another bowl
4. Place the flour in a separate bowl
5. Place the fish into a food processor and add the lemon juice, salt, pepper thyme and mixed herbs
6. Blitz to create a crumb-like consistency
7. Roll your fish in the flour, then the egg and then the breadcrumbs
8. Cook at 180ºC for 8 minutes

Sea Bass With Asparagus Spears

Servings: 2
Cooking Time:xx

Ingredients:

- 2 x 100-g/3½-oz. sea bass fillets
- 8 asparagus spears
- 2 teaspoons olive oil
- salt and freshly ground black pepper
- boiled new potatoes, to serve
- CAPER DRESSING
- 1½ tablespoons olive oil
- grated zest and freshly squeezed juice of ½ lemon
- 1 tablespoon small, jarred capers
- 1 teaspoon Dijon mustard
- 1 tablespoon freshly chopped flat-leaf parsley

Directions:

1. Preheat the air-fryer to 180ºC/350ºF.
2. Prepare the fish and asparagus by brushing both with the olive oil and sprinkling over salt and pepper.
3. Add the asparagus to the preheated air-fryer and air-fry for 4 minutes, then turn the asparagus and add the fish to the air-fryer drawer. Cook for a further 4 minutes. Check the internal temperature of the fish has reached at least 60ºC/140ºF using a meat thermometer – if not, cook for another minute.
4. Meanwhile, make the dressing by combining all the ingredients in a jar and shaking well. Pour the dressing over the cooked fish and asparagus spears and serve with new potatoes.

Tilapia Fillets

Servings: 2
Cooking Time:xx

Ingredients:

- 2 tbsp melted butter
- 150g almond flour
- 3 tbsp mayonnaise
- 2tilapia fillets
- 25g thinly sliced almonds
- Salt and pepper to taste
- Vegetable oil spray

Directions:

1. Mix the almond flour, butter, pepper and salt together in a bowl
2. Spread mayonnaise on both sides of the fish
3. Cover the fillets in the almond flour mix
4. Spread one side of the fish with the sliced almonds
5. Spray the air fryer with the vegetable spray
6. Place in the air fryer and cook at 160ºC for 10 minutes

Thai-style Tuna Fishcakes

Servings: 2
Cooking Time:xx

Ingredients:

- 200 g/7 oz. cooked potato
- 145 g/5 oz. canned tuna, drained
- 60 g/1 cup canned sweetcorn/corn kernels (drained weight)
- ½ teaspoon soy sauce
- ½ teaspoon fish sauce
- ½ teaspoon Thai 7 spice
- freshly squeezed juice of ½ a lime
- 1 teaspoon freshly grated garlic
- 1 teaspoon freshly grated ginger
- avocado or olive oil, for brushing
- LIME-ALMOND SATAY SAUCE
- 20 ml/4 teaspoons fresh lime juice
- 2 heaped tablespoons almond butter
- 1 teaspoon soy sauce
- ½ teaspoon freshly grated ginger
- ½ teaspoon freshly grated garlic
- ½ teaspoon avocado or olive oil
- ½ teaspoon maple syrup

Directions:

1. Combine all the fishcake ingredients in a food processor and blend together. Divide the mixture into 6 equal portions and mould into fishcakes. Brush a little oil over the top surface of the fishcakes.
2. Preheat the air-fryer to 180ºC/350ºF.
3. Place the fishcakes on an air-fryer liner or a piece of pierced parchment paper and add to the preheated air-fryer. Air-fry for 4 minutes, then turn over and brush the other side of each fishcake with oil and air-fry for a further 4 minutes.
4. To make the satay dipping sauce, mix all ingredients in a bowl with 1 tablespoon warm water. Serve alongside the fishcakes.

Air Fryer Mussels

Servings: 2
Cooking Time:xx

Ingredients:

- 400g mussels
- 1 tbsp butter
- 200ml water
- 1 tsp basil
- 2 tsp minced garlic
- 1 tsp chives
- 1 tsp parsley

Directions:

1. Preheat air fryer to 200ºC
2. Clean the mussels, soak for 30 minutes, and remove the beard
3. Add all ingredients to an air fryer-safe pan
4. Cook for 3 minutes
5. Check to see if the mussels have opened, if not cook for a further 2 minutes. Once all mussels are open, they are ready to eat.

Fish Taco Cauliflower Rice Bowls

Servings: 2
Cooking Time:xx
Ingredients:

- 400g fish of your choice, cut into strips
- 1 tsp chilli powder
- ½ tsp paprika
- 1 sliced avocado
- 25g pickled red onions
- 25g reduced fat sour cream
- ½ tsp cumin
- Salt and pepper to taste
- 300g cauliflower rice
- 1 tbsp lime juice
- 25g fresh coriander
- 1 tbsp sriracha

Directions:

1. Sprinkle both sides of the fish with chilli powder, cumin, paprika, salt and pepper
2. Heat the air fryer to 200ºC, cook the fish for about 12 minutes
3. cook the cauliflower rice according to instructions, mix in lime juice and coriander once cooked
4. Divide the cauliflower rice between two bowls, add the sliced avocado, fish and pickled red onions.
5. Mix the sour cream with the sriracha and drizzle over the top

Peppery Lemon Shrimp

Servings: 2
Cooking Time:xx
Ingredients:

- 300g uncooked shrimp
- 1 tbsp olive oil
- 1 the juice of 1 lemon
- 0.25 tsp garlic powder
- 1 sliced lemon
- 1 tsp pepper
- 0.25 tsp paprika

Directions:

1. Heat the fryer to 200ºC
2. Take a medium sized mixing bowl and combine the lemon juice, pepper, garlic powder, paprika and the olive oil together
3. Add the shrimp to the bowl and make sure they're well coated
4. Arrange the shrimp into the basket of the fryer
5. Cook for between 6-8 minutes, until firm and pink

Thai Salmon Patties

Servings: 7
Cooking Time:xx

Ingredients:

- 1 large can of salmon, drained and bones removed
- 30g panko breadcrumbs
- ¼ tsp salt
- 1 ½ tbsp Thai red curry paste
- 1 ½ tbsp brown sugar
- Zest of 1 lime
- 2 eggs
- Cooking spray

Directions:

1. Take a large bowl and combine all ingredients together until smooth
2. Use your hands to create patties that are around 1 inch in thickness
3. Preheat your air fryer to 180ºC
4. Coat the patties with cooking spray
5. Cook for 4 minutes each side

Coconut Shrimp

Servings: 4
Cooking Time:xx

Ingredients:

- 250g flour
- 1 ½ tsp black pepper
- 2 eggs
- 150g unsweetened flaked coconut
- 1 Serrano chilli, thinly sliced
- 25g panko bread crumbs
- 300g shrimp raw
- ½ tsp salt
- 4 tbsp honey
- 25ml lime juice

Directions:

1. Mix together flour and pepper, in another bowl beat the eggs and in another bowl mix the panko and coconut
2. Dip each of the shrimp in the flour mix then the egg and then cover in the coconut mix
3. Coat the shrimp in cooking spray
4. Place in the air fryer and cook at 200ºC for 6-8 mins turning half way through
5. Mix together the honey, lime juice and chilli and serve with the shrimp

Shrimp Wrapped With Bacon

Servings: 2
Cooking Time:xx

Ingredients:

- 16 shrimp
- 16 slices of bacon
- 2 tbsp ranch dressing to serve

Directions:

1. Preheat the air fryer to 200ºC
2. Wrap the shrimps in the bacon
3. Refrigerate for 30 minutes
4. Cook the shrimp for about 5 minutes turn them over and cook for a further 2 minutes
5. Serve with the ranch dressing on the side

Air Fried Scallops

Servings: 2
Cooking Time:xx

Ingredients:

- 6 scallops
- 1 tbsp olive oil
- Salt and pepper to taste

Directions:

1. Brush the filets with olive oil
2. Sprinkle with salt and pepper
3. Place in the air fryer and cook at 200ºC for 2 mins
4. Turn the scallops over and cook for another 2 minutes

Tandoori Salmon

Servings: 4
Cooking Time:xx

Ingredients:

- 300g salmon
- 1 tbsp butter
- 1 tbsp tandoori spice
- Salt and pepper to taste
- 1 small tomato
- Half a red onion
- 600g plain yogurt
- 30 fresh mint leaves, chopped
- 1 tsp minced green chilli
- 1 tbsp ground cumin
- Half a cucumber, chopped

Directions:

1. Cut the salmon into cubes and coat in the tandoori spice mix. Chill for 30 minutes to marinate
2. Blend mint, cumin and chilli with ¼ of the yogurt refrigerate and leave to steep
3. Peel the tomato and cut into cubes. Peel the cucumber and chop into cubes, finely dice the onion
4. Cook the salmon in the air fryer for 5-6 minutes at 200ºC
5. Mix the flavoured yogurt with the remaining yogurt, tomato, cucumber and onion
6. Place the sauce in serving bowls and place the salmon on top

Crunchy Fish

Servings: 4
Cooking Time:xx

Ingredients:

- 200g dry breadcrumbs
- 4 tbsp olive oil
- 4 fillets of white fish
- 1 beaten egg
- 1 sliced lemon

Directions:

1. Heat the fryer to 180ºC
2. In a medium mixing bowl, combine the olive oil and the breadcrumbs
3. Take the fish and first dip it into the egg and then the breadcrumbs, making sure they are evenly coated well
4. Arrange the fish into the basket
5. Cook for 12 minutes
6. Remove and serve with lemon slices

Vegetarian & Vegan Recipes

Jackfruit Taquitos

Servings: 2
Cooking Time:xx
Ingredients:

- 1 large Jackfruit
- 250g red beans
- 100g pico de gallo sauce
- 50ml water
- 2 tbsp water
- 4 wheat tortillas
- Olive oil spray

Directions:

1. Place the jackfruit, red beans, sauce and water in a saucepan
2. Bring to the boil and simmer for 25 minutes
3. Preheat the air fryer to 185ºC
4. Mash the jackfruit mixture, add ¼ cup of the mix to each tortilla and roll up tightly
5. Spray with olive oil and place in the air fryer
6. Cook for 8 minutes

Roast Cauliflower & Broccoli

Servings: 6
Cooking Time:xx
Ingredients:

- 300g broccoli
- 300g cauliflower
- 2 tbsp oil
- ½ tsp garlic powder
- ¼ tsp salt
- ¼ tsp paprika
- ⅛ tsp pepper

Directions:

1. Preheat air fryer to 200ºC
2. Place broccoli and cauliflower in a bowl and microwave for 3 minutes
3. Add remaining ingredients and mix well
4. Add to the air fryer and cook for about 12 mins

Artichoke Crostini

Servings: 2
Cooking Time:xx
Ingredients:

- 100g cashews
- 1 tbsp olive oil
- 1 tbsp lemon juice
- 1 tsp balsamic vinegar
- 3 tbsp hummus
- 200g grilled artichoke hearts
- ½ tsp basil
- ½ tsp oregano
- ⅛ tsp onion powder
- 1 clove garlic minced
- Salt
- 1 baguette cut in ½ inch slices

Directions:

1. Combine cashews, olive oil, lemon juice, balsamic vinegar, basil oregano, onion powder, garlic and salt in a bowl. Set aside
2. Place the baguette slices in the air fryer and cook at 180ºC for 3-4 minutes
3. Sprinkle the baguette slices with cashew mix then add the artichoke hearts
4. Serve with hummus

Roast Vegetables

Servings: 4
Cooking Time:xx
Ingredients:

- 100g diced courgette
- 100g diced squash
- 100g diced mushrooms
- 100g diced cauliflower
- 100g diced asparagus
- 100g diced pepper
- 2 tsp oil
- ½ tsp salt
- ¼ tsp pepper
- ¼ tsp seasoning

Directions:

1. Preheat air fryer to 180ºC
2. Mix all ingredients together
3. Add to air fryer and cook for 10 minutes stirring halfway

Whole Wheat Pizza

Servings: 2
Cooking Time:xx

Ingredients:

- 100g marinara sauce
- 2 whole wheat pitta
- 200g baby spinach leaves
- 1 small plum tomato, sliced
- 1 clove garlic, sliced
- 400g grated cheese
- 50g shaved parmesan

Directions:

1. Preheat air fryer to 160ºC
2. Spread each of the pitta with marinara sauce
3. Sprinkle with cheese, top with spinach, plum tomato and garlic. Finish with parmesan shavings
4. Place in the air fryer and cook for about 4 mins cheese has melted

Macaroni & Cheese Quiche

Servings: 4
Cooking Time:xx

Ingredients:

- 8 tbsp macaroni pasta
- 1 block of short crust pastry
- 2 tbsp Greek yogurt
- 2 eggs
- 150ml milk
- 1 tsp garlic puree
- 400g grated cheese

Directions:

1. Rub the inside of 4 ramekins with flour
2. Line the ramekins with the pastry
3. Mix the yogurt, garlic and macaroni. Add to the ramekins until ¾ full
4. Mix the egg and milk together and pour over the macaroni. Sprinkle with cheese
5. Heat the air fryer to 180ºC and cook for 20 minutes until golden brown.

Flat Mushroom Pizzas

Servings: 1
Cooking Time:xx

Ingredients:

- 2 portobello mushrooms, cleaned and stalk removed
- 6 mozzarella balls
- 1 teaspoon olive oil
- PIZZA SAUCE
- 100 g/3½ oz. passata/strained tomatoes
- 1 teaspoon dried oregano
- ¼ teaspoon garlic salt

Directions:

1. Preheat the air-fryer to 180ºC/350ºF.
2. Mix the ingredients for the pizza sauce together in a small bowl. Fill each upturned portobello mushroom with sauce, then top each with three mozzarella balls and drizzle the olive oil over.
3. Add the mushrooms to the preheated air-fryer and air-fry for 8 minutes. Serve immediately.

Mushroom Pasta

Servings: 4
Cooking Time:xx
Ingredients:

- 250g sliced mushrooms
- 1 chopped onion
- 2 tsp minced garlic
- 1 tsp salt
- ½ tsp red pepper flakes
- 75g cup cream
- 70g mascarpone
- 1 tsp dried thyme
- 1 tsp ground black pepper
- ½ cup grated parmesan

Directions:

1. Place all the ingredients in a bowl and mix well
2. Heat the air fryer to 175ºC
3. Grease a 7x3 inch pan and pour in the mixture
4. Place in the air fryer and cook for 15 minutes stirring halfway through
5. Pour over cooked pasta and sprinkle with parmesan

Tomato And Herb Tofu

Servings:4
Cooking Time:10 Minutes
Ingredients:

- 1 x 400 g / 14 oz block firm tofu
- 1 tbsp soy sauce
- 2 tbsp tomato paste
- 1 tsp dried oregano
- 1 tsp dried basil
- 1 tsp garlic powder

Directions:

1. Remove the tofu from the packaging and place on a sheet of kitchen roll. Place another sheet of kitchen roll on top of the tofu and place a plate on top of it.
2. Use something heavy to press the plate down on top of the tofu. Leave for 10 minutes to press the water out of the tofu.
3. Remove the paper towels from the tofu and chop them into even slices that are around ½ cm thick.
4. Preheat the air fryer to 180 °C / 350 °F. Remove the mesh basket from the air fryer machine and line with parchment paper.
5. Place the tofu slices on a lined baking sheet.
6. In a bowl, mix the soy sauce, tomato paste, dried oregano, dried basil, and garlic powder until fully combined.
7. Spread the mixture evenly over the tofu slices. Place the tofu slices on the baking sheet in the lined air fryer basket and cook for 10 minutes until the tofu is firm and crispy.
8. Serve the tofu slices with a side of rice or noodles and some hot vegetables.

Roasted Cauliflower

Servings: 2
Cooking Time:xx

Ingredients:

- 3 cloves garlic
- 1 tbsp peanut oil
- ½ tsp salt
- ½ tsp paprika
- 400g cauliflower florets

Directions:

1. Preheat air fryer to 200ºC
2. Crush the garlic, place all ingredients in a bowl and mix well
3. Place in the air fryer and cook for about 15 minutes, shaking every 5 minutes

Parmesan Truffle Oil Fries

Servings: 2
Cooking Time:xx

Ingredients:

- 3 large potatoes, peeled and cut
- 2 tbsp truffle oil
- 2 tbsp grated parmesan
- 1 tsp paprika
- 1 tbsp parsley
- Salt and pepper to taste

Directions:

1. Coat the potatoes with truffle oil and sprinkle with seasonings
2. Add the fries to the air fryer
3. Cook at 180ºC for about 15 minutes shake halfway through
4. Sprinkle with parmesan and parsley to serve

Aubergine Parmigiana

Servings: 2 As A Main Or 4 As A Side
Cooking Time:xx

Ingredients:

- 2 small or 1 large aubergine/eggplant, sliced 5 mm/¼ in. thick
- 1 tablespoon olive oil
- ¾ teaspoon salt
- 200 g/7 oz. mozzarella, sliced
- ½ teaspoon freshly ground black pepper
- 20 g/¼ cup finely grated Parmesan
- green vegetables, to serve
- SAUCE
- 135 g/5 oz. passata/strained tomatoes
- 1 teaspoon dried oregano
- ¼ teaspoon garlic salt
- 1 tablespoon olive oil

Directions:

1. Preheat the air-fryer to 200ºC/400ºF.
2. Rub each of the aubergine/eggplant slices with olive oil and salt. Divide the slices into two batches. Place one batch of the aubergine slices in the preheated air-fryer and air-fry for 4 minutes on one side, then turn over and air-fry for 2 minutes on the other side. Lay these on the base of a gratin dish that fits into your air-fryer.
3. Air-fry the second batch of aubergine slices in the same way. Whilst they're cooking, mix together the sauce ingredients in a small bowl.
4. Spread the sauce over the aubergines in the gratin dish. Add a layer of the mozzarella slices, then season with pepper. Add a second layer of aubergine slices, then top with Parmesan.
5. Place the gratin dish in the air-fryer and air-fry for 6 minutes, until the mozzarella is melted and the top of the dish is golden brown. Serve immediately with green vegetables on the side.

Falafel Burgers

Servings: 2
Cooking Time:xx

Ingredients:

- 1 large can of chickpeas
- 1 onion
- 1 lemon
- 140g oats
- 28g grated cheese
- 28g feta cheese
- Salt and pepper to taste
- 3 tbsp Greek yogurt
- 4 tbsp soft cheese
- 1 tbsp garlic puree
- 1 tbsp coriander
- 1 tbsp oregano
- 1 tbsp parsley

Directions:

1. Place the chickpeas, onion, lemon rind, garlic and seasonings and blend until coarse
2. Add the mix to a bowl and stir in half the soft cheese, cheese and feta
3. Form in to burger shape and coat in the oats
4. Place in the air fryer and cook at 180ºC for 8 minutes
5. To make the sauce mix the remaining soft cheese, greek yogurt and lemon juice in a bowl

Gnocchi Caprese

Servings: 2
Cooking Time:xx

Ingredients:

- 1 packet of gnocchi
- 150g cherry tomatoes, cut into halves
- 2 tbsp olive oil
- 2 tbsp balsamic vinegar
- 3 pressed cloves of garlic
- 200g basil, chopped
- 200g mini mozzarella balls
- 150g grated Parmesan
- Salt and pepper for seasoning

Directions:

1. Preheat the air fryer to 220ºC
2. Take a large bowl and add the cherry tomatoes, gnocchi, oil, balsamic vinegar, garlic and seasoning, making sure that everything is well coated
3. Transfer to the air fryer basket
4. Cook for 10 minutes, shaking the basket every few minutes
5. Once cooked, transfer everything to a large mixing bowl and add the Parmesan cheese, coating well
6. Then, add the mozzarella and basil and toss once more

Baked Feta, Tomato & Garlic Pasta

Servings: 2
Cooking Time:xx

Ingredients:

- 100 g/3½ oz. feta or plant-based feta, cubed
- 20 cherry tomatoes
- 2 garlic cloves, peeled and halved
- ¾ teaspoon oregano
- 1 teaspoon chilli/hot red pepper flakes
- ½ teaspoon garlic salt
- 2 tablespoons olive oil
- 100 g/3½ oz. cooked pasta plus about 1 tablespoon of cooking water
- freshly ground black pepper

Directions:

1. Preheat the air-fryer to 200ºC/400ºF.
2. Place the feta, tomatoes and garlic in a baking dish that fits inside your air-fryer. Top with the oregano, chilli/hot red pepper flakes, garlic salt and olive oil. Place the dish in the preheated air-fryer and air-fry for 10 minutes, then remove and stir in the pasta and cooking water. Serve sprinkled with black pepper.

Rainbow Vegetables

Servings: 4
Cooking Time:xx

Ingredients:

- 1 red pepper, cut into slices
- 1 squash sliced
- 1 courgette sliced
- 1 tbsp olive oil
- 150g sliced mushrooms
- 1 onion sliced
- Salt and pepper to taste

Directions:

1. Preheat air fryer to 180ºC
2. Place all ingredients in a bowl and mix well
3. Place in the air fryer and cook for about 20 minutes turning halfway

Courgette Burgers

Servings: 4
Cooking Time:xx

Ingredients:

- 1 courgette
- 1 small can of chickpeas, drained
- 3 spring onions
- Pinch of dried garlic
- Salt and pepper
- 3 tbsp coriander
- 1 tsp chilli powder
- 1 tsp mixed spice
- 1 tsp cumin

Directions:

1. Grate the courgette and drain the excess water
2. Thinly slice the spring onions and add to the bowl with the chickpeas, courgette and seasoning
3. Bind the ingredients and form into patties
4. Place in the air fryer and cook for 12 minutes at 200ºC

Radish Hash Browns

Servings: 4
Cooking Time:xx

Ingredients:

- 300g radish
- 1 onion
- 1 tsp onion powder
- ¾ tsp sea salt
- ½ tsp paprika
- ¼ tsp ground black pepper
- 1 tsp coconut oil

Directions:

1. Wash the radish, trim off the roots and slice in a processor along with the onions
2. Add the coconut oil and mix well
3. Put the onions and radish into the air fryer and cook at 180ºC for 8 minutes shaking a few times
4. Put the onion and radish in a bowl add seasoning and mix well
5. Put back in the air fryer and cook at 200ºC for 5 minutes

Satay Tofu Skewers

Servings: 2
Cooking Time:xx

Ingredients:

- 300 g/10½ oz. firm tofu
- Lime-Almond Satay Sauce (see page 87), to serve
- MARINADE
- 200 ml/¾ cup coconut milk (including the thick part from the can)
- 1 plump garlic clove, finely chopped
- 2 teaspoons grated ginger
- 2 tablespoons soy sauce
- 1 heaped tablespoon smooth peanut butter
- 1 tablespoon maple syrup
- 1 tablespoon mild curry powder
- 1 tablespoon fish sauce or plant-based alternative

Directions:

1. Cut the tofu into 2 x 2-cm/¾ x ¾-in. cubes. Mix the marinade ingredients thoroughly, then toss in the tofu cubes. Once the tofu cubes are covered in the marinade, leave in the fridge to marinate for at least 4 hours.
2. Preheat the air-fryer to 180ºC/350ºF.
3. Thread the tofu cubes onto 4 skewers that fit inside your air-fryer. Place on an air-fryer liner or a piece of pierced parchment paper and add to the preheated air-fryer. Air-fry for 12 minutes, turning over once during cooking.
4. Serve the tofu skewers alongside a bowl of the Lime-Almond Satay Sauce.

Air-fried Artichoke Hearts

Servings: 7
Cooking Time:xx

Ingredients:

- 14 artichoke hearts
- 200g flour
- ¼ tsp baking powder
- Salt
- 6 tbsp water
- 6 tbsp breadcrumbs
- ¼ tsp basil
- ¼ tsp oregano
- ¼ tsp garlic powder
- ¼ tsp paprika

Directions:

1. Mix the baking powder, salt, flour and water in a bowl
2. In another bowl combine the breadcrumbs and seasonings
3. Dip the artichoke in the batter then coat in breadcrumbs
4. Place in the air fryer and cook at 180ºC for 8 minutes

Side Dishes Recipes

Zingy Brussels Sprouts

Servings: 2
Cooking Time:xx
Ingredients:

- 1 tbsp avocado oil
- ½ tsp salt
- ½ tsp pepper
- 400g Brussels sprouts halved
- 1 tsp balsamic vinegar
- 2 tsp crumbled bacon

Directions:

1. Preheat air fryer to 175ºC
2. Combine oil, salt and pepper in a bowl and mix well. Add Brussels sprouts
3. Place in the air fryer and cook for 5 minutes shake then cook for another 5 minutes
4. Sprinkle with balsamic vinegar and sprinkle with bacon

Stuffing Filled Pumpkin

Servings: 2
Cooking Time:xx
Ingredients:

- 1/2 small pumpkin
- 1 diced parsnip
- 1 sweet potato, diced
- 1 diced onion
- 2 tsp dried mixed herbs
- 50g peas
- 1 carrot, diced
- 1 egg
- 2 minced garlic cloves

Directions:

1. Remove the seeds from the pumpkin
2. Combine all the other ingredients in a bowl
3. Stuff the pumpkin
4. Preheat the air fryer to 175ºC
5. Place the pumpkin in the air fryer and cook for about 30 minutes

Hasselback New Potatoes

Servings: 4
Cooking Time:xx
Ingredients:

- 8–12 new potatoes, roughly 5–7 cm/2–2¾ in. in length
- 2 teaspoons olive oil
- salt
- 1 tablespoon butter (optional)

Directions:

1. Preheat the air-fryer to 180ºC/350ºF.
2. Slice the potatoes multiple times widthways, making sure you do not cut all the way through (if you place the potatoes in the bowl of a wooden spoon to make these slices, it prevents you cutting all the way through). Coat the potatoes in the olive oil and sprinkle over the salt.
3. Add the potatoes to the preheated air-fryer and air-fry for 20–25 minutes until the potatoes are crispy on the outside but soft on the inside. Serve immediately.

Crispy Sweet & Spicy Cauliflower

Servings: 2
Cooking Time:xx

Ingredients:

- ½ a head of cauliflower
- 1 teaspoon sriracha sauce
- 1 teaspoon soy sauce (or tamari)
- ½ teaspoon maple syrup
- 2 teaspoons olive oil or avocado oil

Directions:

1. Preheat the air-fryer to 180ºC/350ºF.
2. Chop the cauliflower into florets with a head size of roughly 5 cm/1 in. Place the other ingredients in a bowl and mix together, then add the florets and toss to coat them.
3. Add the cauliflower to the preheated air-fryer and air-fry for 12 minutes, shaking the drawer a couple of times during cooking.

Alternative Stuffed Potatoes

Servings: 4
Cooking Time:xx

Ingredients:

- 4 baking potatoes, peeled and halved
- 1 tbsp olive oil
- 150g grated cheese
- ½ onion, diced
- 2 slices bacon

Directions:

1. Preheat air fryer to 175ºC
2. Brush the potatoes with oil and cook in the air fryer for 10 minutes
3. Coat again with oil and cook for a further 10 minutes
4. Cut the potatoes in half spoon the insides into a bowl and mix in the cheese
5. Place the bacon and onion in a pan and cook until browned, mix in with the potato
6. Stuff the skins with the mix and return to the air fryer, cook for about 6 minutes

Yorkshire Puddings

Servings: 2
Cooking Time:xx

Ingredients:

- 1 tablespoon olive oil
- 70 g/½ cup plus ½ tablespoon plain/all-purpose flour (gluten-free if you wish)
- 100 ml/7 tablespoons milk
- 2 eggs
- salt and freshly ground black pepper

Directions:

1. You will need 4 ramekins. Preheat the air-fryer to 200ºC/400ºF.
2. Using a pastry brush, oil the base and sides of each ramekin, dividing the oil equally between the ramekins. Place the greased ramekins in the preheated air-fryer and heat for 5 minutes.
3. Meanwhile, in a food processor or using a whisk, combine the flour, milk, eggs and seasoning until you have a batter that is frothy on top. Divide the batter equally between the preheated ramekins. Return the ramekins to the air-fryer and air-fry for 20 minutes without opening the drawer. Remove the Yorkshire puddings from the ramekins and serve immediately.

Aubergine Parmesan

Servings: 4
Cooking Time:xx

Ingredients:

- 100g Italian breadcrumbs
- 50g grated parmesan
- 1 tsp Italian seasoning
- 1 tsp salt
- ½ tsp dried basil
- ½ tsp onion powder
- ½ tsp black pepper
- 100g flour
- 2 eggs
- 1 aubergine, sliced into ½ inch rounds

Directions:

1. Mix breadcrumbs, parmesan, salt Italian seasoning, basil, onion powder and pepper in a bowl
2. Add the flour to another bowl, and beat the eggs in another
3. Dip the aubergine in the flour, then the eggs and then coat in the bread crumbs
4. Preheat the air fryer to 185ºC
5. Place the aubergine in the air fryer and cook for 8-10 minutes
6. Turnover and cook for a further 4-6 minutes

Super Easy Fries

Servings: 2
Cooking Time:xx

Ingredients:

- 500g potatoes cut into ½ inch sticks
- 1 tsp olive oil
- ¼ tsp salt
- ¼ tsp pepper

Directions:

1. Place the potatoes in a bowl cover with water and allow to soak for 30 minutes
2. Spread the butter onto one side of the bread slices
3. Pat dry with paper, drizzle with oil and toss to coat
4. Place in the air fryer and cook at 200ºC for about 15 minutes, keep tossing through cooking time
5. Sprinkle with salt and pepper

Air Fryer Corn On The Cob

Servings: 2
Cooking Time:xx

Ingredients:

- 2 corn on the cob
- 2 tbsp melted butter
- A pinch of salt
- 1/2 tsp dried parsley
- 2 tbsp grated parmesan

Directions:

1. Preheat the air fryer to 270ºC
2. Take a bowl and combine the melted butter, salt and parsley
3. Brush the corn with the mixture
4. Add the corn inside the air fryer and cook for 14 minutes
5. Remove the corn from the fryer and roll in the grated cheese

Butternut Squash

Servings: 4
Cooking Time:xx

Ingredients:

- 500 g/1 lb. 2 oz. butternut squash, chopped into 2.5-cm/1-in. cubes
- 1 tablespoon olive oil or avocado oil
- 1 teaspoon smoked paprika
- 1 teaspoon dried oregano
- ½ teaspoon salt
- ¼ teaspoon freshly ground black pepper

Directions:

1. Preheat the air-fryer to 180ºC/350ºF.
2. In a bowl toss the butternut squash cubes in the oil and all the seasonings.
3. Add the butternut squash cubes to the preheated air-fryer and air-fry for 16–18 minutes, shaking the drawer once during cooking.

Roasted Okra

Servings: 1
Cooking Time:xx

Ingredients:

- 300g Okra, ends trimmed and pods sliced
- 1 tsp olive oil
- ¼ tsp salt
- ⅛ tsp pepper

Directions:

1. Preheat the air fryer to 175°C
2. Combine all ingredients in a bowl and stir gently
3. Place in the air fryer and cook for 5 minutes, shake and cook for another 5 minutes

Egg Fried Rice

Servings:2
Cooking Time:15 Minutes

Ingredients:

- 400 g / 14 oz cooked white or brown rice
- 100 g / 3.5 oz fresh peas and sweetcorn
- 2 tbsp olive oil
- 2 eggs, scrambled

Directions:

1. Preheat the air fryer to 150 °C / 300 °F and line the bottom of the basket with parchment paper.
2. In a bowl, mix the cooked white or brown rice and the fresh peas and sweetcorn.
3. Pour in 2 tbsp olive oil and toss to coat evenly. Stir in the scrambled eggs.
4. Transfer the egg rice into the lined air fryer basket, close the lid, and cook for 15 minutes until the eggs are cooked and the rice is soft.
5. Serve as a side dish with some cooked meat or tofu.

Orange Sesame Cauliflower

Servings: 4
Cooking Time:xx

Ingredients:

- 100ml water
- 30g cornstarch
- 50g flour
- 1/2 tsp salt
- ½ tsp pepper
- 2 tbsp tomato ketchup
- 2 tbsp brown sugar
- 1 sliced onion

Directions:

1. Mix together flour, cornstarch, water, salt and pepper until smooth
2. Coat the cauliflower and chill for 30 minutes
3. Place in the air fryer and cook for 22 minutes at 170ºC
4. Meanwhile combine remaining ingredients in a saucepan, gently simmer until thickened.
5. Mix cauliflower with sauce and top with toasted sesame seeds to serve

Pumpkin Fries

Servings: 4
Cooking Time:xx

Ingredients:

- 1 small pumpkin, seeds removed and peeled, cut into half inch slices
- 2 tsp olive oil
- 1 tsp garlic powder
- 1/2 tsp paprika
- A pinch of salt

Directions:

1. Take a large bowl and add the slices of pumpkin
2. Add the oil and all the seasonings. Toss to coat well
3. Place in the air fryer
4. Cook at 280ºC for 15 minutes, until the chips are tender, shaking at the halfway point

Honey Roasted Parsnips

Servings: 4
Cooking Time:xx

Ingredients:

- 350 g/12 oz. parsnips
- 1 tablespoon plain/all-purpose flour (gluten-free if you wish)
- 1½ tablespoons runny honey
- 2 tablespoons olive oil
- salt

Directions:

1. Top and tail the parsnips, then slice lengthways, about 2 cm/¾ in. wide. Place in a saucepan with water to cover and a good pinch of salt. Bring to the boil, then boil for 5 minutes.
2. Remove and drain well, allowing any excess water to evaporate. Dust the parsnips with flour. Mix together the honey and oil in a small bowl, then toss in the parsnips to coat well in the honey and oil.
3. Preheat the air-fryer to 180ºC/350ºF.
4. Add the parsnips to the preheated air-fryer and air-fry for 14–16 minutes, depending on how dark you like the outsides (the longer you cook them, the sweeter they get).

Crispy Broccoli

Servings: 2
Cooking Time:xx
Ingredients:

- 170 g/6 oz. broccoli florets
- 2 tablespoons olive oil
- ⅛ teaspoon garlic salt
- ⅛ teaspoon freshly ground black pepper
- 2 tablespoons freshly grated Parmesan or Pecorino

Directions:

1. Preheat the air-fryer to 200ºC/400ºF.
2. Toss the broccoli in the oil, season with the garlic salt and pepper, then toss over the grated cheese and combine well. Add the broccoli to the preheated air-fryer and air-fry for 5 minutes, giving the broccoli a stir halfway through to ensure even cooking.

Tex Mex Hash Browns

Servings: 4
Cooking Time:xx
Ingredients:

- 500g potatoes cut into cubes
- 1 tbsp olive oil
- 1 red pepper
- 1 onion
- 1 jalapeño pepper
- ½ tsp taco seasoning
- ½ tsp cumin
- Salt and pepper to taste

Directions:

1. Soak the potatoes in water for 20 minutes
2. Heat the air fryer to 160ºC
3. Drain the potatoes and coat with olive oil
4. Add to the air fryer and cook for 18 minutes
5. Mix the remaining ingredients in a bowl, add the potatoes and mix well
6. Place the mix into the air fryer cook for 6 minutes, shake and cook for a further 5 minutes

Garlic And Parsley Potatoes

Servings: 4
Cooking Time:xx
Ingredients:

- 500g baby potatoes, cut into quarters
- 1 tbsp oil
- 1 tsp salt
- ½ tsp garlic powder
- ½ tsp dried parsley

Directions:

1. Preheat air fryer to 175ºC
2. Combine potatoes and oil in a bowl
3. Add remaining ingredients and mix
4. Add to the air fryer and cook for about 25 minutes until golden brown, turning halfway through

Mexican Rice

Servings: 4
Cooking Time:xx

Ingredients:

- 500g long grain rice
- 3 tbsp olive oil
- 60ml water
- 1 tsp chilli powder
- 1/4 tsp cumin
- 2 tbsp tomato paste
- 1/2 tsp garlic powder
- 1tsp red pepper flakes
- 1 chopped onion
- 500ml chicken stock
- Half a small jalapeño pepper with seeds out, chopped
- Salt for seasoning

Directions:

1. Add the water and tomato paste and combine, placing to one side
2. Take a baking pan and add a little oil
3. Wash the rice and add to the baking pan
4. Add the chicken stock, tomato paste, jalapeños, onions, and the rest of the olive oil, and combine
5. Place aluminium foil over the top and place in your air fryer
6. Cook at 220ºC for 50 minutes
7. Keep checking the rice as it cooks, as the liquid should be absorbing

Celery Root Fries

Servings: 2
Cooking Time:xx

Ingredients:

- ½ celeriac, cut into sticks
- 500ml water
- 1 tbsp lime juice
- 1 tbsp olive oil
- 75g mayo
- 1 tbsp mustard
- 1 tbsp powdered horseradish

Directions:

1. Put celeriac in a bowl, add water and lime juice, soak for 30 minutes
2. Preheat air fryer to 200
3. Mix together the mayo, horseradish powder and mustard, refrigerate
4. Drain the celeriac, drizzle with oil and season with salt and pepper
5. Place in the air fryer and cook for about 10 minutes turning halfway
6. Serve with the mayo mix as a dip

Desserts Recipes

Christmas Biscuits

Servings: 8
Cooking Time:xx

Ingredients:

- 225g self raising flour
- 100g caster sugar
- 100g butter
- Juice and rind of orange
- 1 egg beaten
- 2 tbsp cocoa
- 2 tsp vanilla essence
- 8 pieces dark chocolate

Directions:

1. Preheat the air fryer to 180ºC
2. Rub the butter into the flour. Add the sugar, vanilla, orange and cocoa mix well
3. Add the egg and mix to a dough
4. Split the dough into 8 equal pieces
5. Place a piece of chocolate in each piece of dough and form into a ball covering the chocolate
6. Place in the air fryer and cook for 15 minutes

Chocolate Cake

Servings: 2
Cooking Time:xx

Ingredients:

- 3 eggs
- 75ml sour cream
- 225g flour
- 150g sugar
- 2 tsp vanilla extract
- 25g cocoa powder
- 1 tsp baking powder
- ½ tsp baking soda

Directions:

1. Preheat the air fryer to 160ºC
2. Mix all the ingredients together in a bowl
3. Pour into a greased baking tin
4. Place into the air fryer and cook for 25 minutes
5. Allow to cool and ice with chocolate frosting

Sugar Dough Dippers

Servings: 12
Cooking Time:xx

Ingredients:

- 300g bread dough
- 75g melted butter
- 100g sugar
- 200ml double cream
- 200g semi sweet chocolate
- 2 tbsp amaretto

Directions:

1. Roll the dough into 2 15inch logs, cut each one into 20 slices. Cut each slice in half and twist together 2-3 times. Brush with melted butter and sprinkle with sugar
2. Preheat the air fryer to 150ºC
3. Place dough in the air fryer and cook for 5 minutes, turnover and cook for a further 3 minutes
4. Place the cream in a pan and bring to simmer over a medium heat, place the chocolate chips in a bowl and pour over the cream
5. Mix until the chocolate is melted then stir in the amaretto
6. Serve the dough dippers with the chocolate dip

Chocolate Orange Muffins

Servings: 12
Cooking Time:xx

Ingredients:

- 100g self raising flour
- 110g caster sugar
- 50g butter
- 20g cocoa powder
- 50ml milk
- 1 tsp cocoa nibs
- 1 large orange juice and rind
- 1 tbsp honey
- 1tsp vanilla essence
- 2 eggs

Directions:

1. Add the flour, butter and sugar to a mixing bowl and rug together
2. Add the cocoa, honey, orange and vanilla mix well
3. Mix the milk and egg together then add to the flour mix, combine well
4. Rub your muffin cases with flour to stop them sticking, add 2 tbsp batter to each one
5. Cook in the air fryer for 12 minutes at 180ºC

Coffee, Chocolate Chip, And Banana Bread

Servings:8

Cooking Time:1 Hour 10 Minutes

Ingredients:

- 200 g / 7 oz plain flour
- 1 tsp baking powder
- 1 tsp ground cinnamon
- 1 tbsp ground coffee
- ½ tsp salt
- 2 ripe bananas, peeled
- 2 eggs, beaten
- 100 g / 3.5 oz granulated sugar
- 50 g / 3.5 oz brown sugar
- 100 g / 3.5 oz milk chocolate chips
- 4 tbsp milk
- 2 tbsp olive oil
- 1 tsp vanilla extract

Directions:

1. Preheat the air fryer to 150 °C / 300 °F and line a loaf tin with parchment paper.
2. In a large mixing bowl, combine the plain flour, baking powder, ground cinnamon, and salt.
3. Mash the ripe bananas in a separate bowl until there are no lumps. Whisk in the beaten eggs, followed by the granulated sugar, brown sugar, and milk chocolate chips until well combined.
4. Stir in the milk, olive oil, and vanilla extract before combining the dry and wet ingredients. Mix until combined into one smooth mixture.
5. Pour the batter into the prepared loaf tin and transfer into the air fryer basket. Cook for 30-40 minutes until the cake is set and golden on top. Insert a knife into the centre of the cake. It should come out dry when the cake is fully cooked.
6. Remove the loaf tin from the air fryer and set aside to cool on a drying rack. Once cooled, remove the cake from the loaf tin and cut into slices.
7. Enjoy the cake hot or cold.

Chocolate Eclairs

Servings: 9

Cooking Time:xx

Ingredients:

- 100g plain flour
- 50g butter
- 3 eggs
- 150ml water
- 25g butter
- 1 tsp vanilla extract
- 1 tsp icing sugar
- 150ml whipped cream
- 50g milk chocolate
- 1 tbsp whipped cream

Directions:

1. Preheat the air fryer to 180ºC
2. Add 50g of butter to a pan along with the water and melt over a medium heat
3. Remove from the heat and stir in the flour. Return to the heat until mix form a single ball of dough
4. Allow to cool, once cool beat in the eggs until you have a smooth dough
5. Make into eclair shapes, cook in the air fryer at 180ºC for 10 minutes and then 160ºC for 8 minutes
6. Mix the vanilla, icing sugar and 150ml of whipping cream until nice and thick
7. Once cool fill each eclair with the cream mix
8. Place the chocolate, 1 tbsp whipped cream and 25g of butter in a glass bowl and melt over a pan of boiling water. Top the eclairs

Brownies

Servings: 6
Cooking Time:xx

Ingredients:

- 25g melted butter
- 50g sugar
- 1 egg
- ½ tsp vanilla
- 25g flour
- 3 tbsp cocoa
- ⅛ tsp baking powder
- ⅛ tsp salt

Directions:

1. Preheat the air fryer to 165ºC
2. Add all the wet ingredients to a bowl and combine.
3. Add the dry ingredients and mix well
4. Place the batter into a prepared pan and cook in the air fryer for 13 minutes

Chocolate-glazed Banana Slices

Servings:2
Cooking Time:10 Minutes

Ingredients:

- 2 bananas
- 1 tbsp honey
- 1 tbsp chocolate spread, melted
- 2 tbsp milk chocolate chips

Directions:

1. Preheat the air fryer to 180 °C / 350 °F. Remove the mesh basket from the machine and line it with parchment paper.
2. Cut the two bananas into even slices and place them in the lined air fryer basket.
3. In a small bowl, mix the honey and melted chocolate spread. Use a brush to glaze the banana slices. Carefully press the milk chocolate chips into the banana slices enough so that they won't fall out when you transfer the bananas into the air fryer.
4. Carefully slide the mesh basket into the air fryer, close the lid, and cook for 10 minutes until the bananas are hot and the choc chips have melted.
5. Enjoy the banana slices on their own or with a side of ice cream.

Peanut Butter And Banana Bites

Servings: 12
Cooking Time:xx

Ingredients:

- 1 banana
- 12 wonton wrappers
- 75g peanut butter
- 1-2 tsp vegetable oil

Directions:

1. Slice the banana and place in a bowl of water with lemon juice to prevent browning
2. Place one piece of banana and a spoon of peanut butter in each wonton wrapper
3. Wet the edges of each wrapper and fold over to seal
4. Spray the air fryer with oil
5. Place in the air fryer and cook at 190ºC for 6 minutes

Brazilian Pineapple

Servings: 2
Cooking Time:xx

Ingredients:

- 1 small pineapple, cut into spears
- 100g brown sugar
- 2 tsp cinnamon
- 3 tbsp melted butter

Directions:

1. Mix the brown sugar and cinnamon together in a small bowl
2. Brush the pineapple with melted butter
3. Sprinkle with the sugar and cinnamon
4. Heat the air fryer to 200ºC
5. Cook the pineapple for about 10 minutes

Apple And Cinnamon Puff Pastry Pies

Servings:8
Cooking Time:20 Minutes

Ingredients:

- 4 tbsp butter
- 4 tbsp white sugar
- 2 tbsp brown sugar
- 1 tsp cinnamon
- 1 tsp nutmeg
- 1 tsp salt
- 4 apples, peeled and diced
- 2 large sheets puff pastry
- 1 egg

Directions:

1. Preheat the air fryer to 180 °C / 350 °F. Remove the mesh basket from the machine and line it with parchment paper.
2. In a bowl, whisk together the butter, white sugar, brown sugar, cinnamon, nutmeg, and salt.
3. Place the apples in a heatproof baking dish and coat them in the butter and sugar mixture. Transfer to the air fryer and cook for 10 minutes.
4. Meanwhile, roll out the pastry on a clean, floured surface. Cut the sheets into 8 equal parts.
5. Once the apples are hot and softened, evenly spread the mixture between the pastry sheets. Fold the sheets over to cover the apple and gently press the edges using a fork or your fingers to seal the mixture in.
6. Beat the egg in a bowl and use a brush to coat the top of each pastry sheet.
7. Carefully transfer the filled pastry sheets to the prepared air fryer basket, close the lid, and cook for 10 minutes until the pastry is golden and crispy.

Milk And White Chocolate Chip Air Fryer Donuts With Frosting

Servings:4

Cooking Time:10 Minutes

Ingredients:

- For the donuts:
- 200 ml milk (any kind)
- 50 g / 3.5 oz brown sugar
- 50 g / 3.5 oz granulated sugar
- 1 tbsp active dry yeast
- 2 tbsp olive oil
- 4 tbsp butter, melted
- 1 egg, beaten
- 1 tsp vanilla extract
- 400 g / 14 oz plain flour
- 4 tbsp cocoa powder
- 100 g / 3.5 oz milk chocolate chips
- For the frosting:
- 5 tbsp powdered sugar
- 2 tbsp cocoa powder
- 100 ml heavy cream
- 50 g / 1.8 oz white chocolate chips, melted

Directions:

1. To make the donuts, whisk together the milk, brown and granulated sugars, and active dry yeast in a bowl. Set aside for a few minutes while the yeast starts to get foamy.
2. Stir the melted butter, beaten egg, and vanilla extract into the bowl. Mix well until all of the ingredients are combined.
3. Fold in the plain flour and cocoa powder until a smooth mixture forms.
4. Lightly flour a clean kitchen top surface and roll the dough out. Gently knead the dough for 2-3 minutes until it becomes soft and slightly tacky.
5. Transfer the dough into a large mixing bowl and cover it with a clean tea towel or some tinfoil. Leave the dough to rise for around one hour in a warm place.
6. Remove the tea towel or tinfoil from the bowl and roll it out on a floured surface once again. Use a rolling pin to roll the dough into a one-inch thick circle.
7. Use a round cookie cutter to create circular donuts and place each one into a lined air fryer basket.
8. Once all of the donuts have been placed into the air fryer, turn the machine onto 150 °C / 300 °F and close the lid.
9. Cook the donuts for 8-10 minutes until they are slightly golden and crispy on the outside.
10. While the donuts are cooking in the air fryer, make the frosting by combining the powdered sugar, cocoa powder, heavy cream, and melted white chocolate chips in a bowl. Mix well until a smooth, sticky mixture forms.
11. When the donuts are cooked, remove them from the air fryer and set aside to cool for 5-10 minutes. Once cooled, evenly spread some frosting on the top layer of each one. Place in the fridge to set for at least one hour.
12. Enjoy the donuts hot or cold.

Spiced Apples

Servings: 4

Cooking Time:xx

Ingredients:

- 4 apples, sliced
- 2 tbsp ghee
- 2 tbsp sugar
- 1 tsp apple pie spice

Directions:

1. Place apples in a bowl, add the ghee and sprinkle with sugar and apple pie spice
2. Place in a tin that will fit the air fryer
3. Heat the air fryer to 175°C
4. Put the tin in the air fryer and cook for 10 minutes until tender

Granola

Servings: 3
Cooking Time:xx

Ingredients:

- 60 g/¼ cup runny honey
- 50 g/3 tablespoons coconut oil
- 1 teaspoon vanilla extract
- 100 g/¾ cup jumbo rolled oats/old-fashioned oats (not porridge oats)
- 50 g/½ cup chopped walnuts
- 1 teaspoon ground cinnamon

Directions:

1. Preheat the air-fryer to 180ºC/350ºF.
2. Place the honey, coconut oil and vanilla extract in a small dish. Add this to the preheated air-fryer for 1 minute to melt.
3. In a small bowl combine the oats, nuts and cinnamon. Add the melted honey mixture and toss well, ensuring all the oats and nuts are well coated.
4. Lay an air-fryer liner or a pierced piece of parchment paper on the base of the air-fryer drawer. Add the granola mix on top, spread evenly in one layer. Air-fry for 4 minutes, then stir before cooking for a further 3 minutes. Leave to cool completely before serving or storing in a jar.

Butter Cake

Servings: 4
Cooking Time:xx

Ingredients:

- Cooking spray
- 7 tbsp butter
- 25g white sugar
- 2 tbsp white sugar
- 1 egg
- 300g flour
- Pinch salt
- 6 tbsp milk

Directions:

1. Preheat air fryer to 175ºC
2. Spray a small fluted tube pan with cooking spray
3. Beat the butter and all of the sugar together in a bowl until creamy
4. Add the egg and mix until fluffy, add the salt and flour mix well. Add the milk and mix well
5. Put the mix in the pan and cook in the air fryer for 15 minutes

Pistachio Brownies

Servings: 4
Cooking Time:xx

Ingredients:

- 75ml milk
- ½ tsp vanilla extract
- 25g salt
- 25g pecans
- 75g flour
- 75g sugar
- 25g cocoa powder
- 1 tbsp ground flax seeds

Directions:

1. Mix all of the dry ingredients together, in another bowl mix the wet ingredients
2. Add all the ingredients together and mix well
3. Preheat the air fryer to 175ºC
4. Line a 5 inch cake tin with parchment paper
5. Pour the brownie mix into the cake tin and cook in the air fryer for about 20 minutes

New York Cheesecake

Servings: 8
Cooking Time:xx

Ingredients:

- 225g plain flour
- 100g brown sugar
- 100g butter
- 50g melted butter
- 1 tbsp vanilla essence
- 750g soft cheese
- 2 cups caster sugar
- 3 large eggs
- 50ml quark

Directions:

1. Add the flour, sugar, and 100g butter to a bowl and mix until combined. Form into biscuit shapes place in the air fryer and cook for 15 minutes at 180ºC
2. Grease a springform tin
3. Break the biscuits up and mix with the melted butter, press firmly into the tin
4. Mix the soft cheese and sugar in a bowl until creamy, add the eggs and vanilla and mix. Mix in the quark
5. Pour the cheesecake batter into the pan
6. Place in your air fryer and cook for 30 minutes at 180ºC. Leave in the air fryer for 30 minutes whilst it cools
7. Refrigerate for 6 hours

Zebra Cake

Servings: 6
Cooking Time:xx

Ingredients:

- 115g butter
- 2 eggs
- 100g caster sugar
- 1 tbsp cocoa powder
- 100g self raising flour
- 30ml milk
- 1tsp vanilla

Directions:

1. Preheat air fryer to 160ºC
2. Line a 6 inch baking tin
3. Beat together the butter and sugar until light and fluffy
4. Add eggs one at a time then add the vanilla and milk
5. Add the flour and mix well
6. Divide the mix in half
7. Add cocoa powder to half the mix and mix well
8. Add a scoop of each of the batters at a time until it's all in the tin, place in the air fryer and cook for 30 minutes

Grilled Ginger & Coconut Pineapple Rings

Servings: 4
Cooking Time:xx

Ingredients:

- 1 medium pineapple
- coconut oil, melted
- 1½ teaspoons coconut sugar
- ½ teaspoon ground ginger
- coconut or vanilla yogurt, to serve

Directions:

1. Preheat the air-fryer to 180ºC/350ºF.
2. Peel and core the pineapple, then slice into 4 thick rings.
3. Mix together the melted coconut oil with the sugar and ginger in a small bowl. Using a pastry brush, paint this mixture all over the pineapple rings, including the sides of the rings.
4. Add the rings to the preheated air-fryer and air-fry for 20 minutes. Check after 18 minutes as pineapple sizes vary and your rings may be perfectly cooked already. You'll know they are ready when they're golden in colour and a fork can easily be inserted with very little resistance
5. Serve warm with a generous spoonful of yogurt.

Special Oreos

Servings: 9
Cooking Time:xx

Ingredients:

- 100g pancake mix
- 25ml water
- Cooking spray
- 9 Oreos
- 1 tbsp icing sugar

Directions:

1. Mix pancake mix and water until well combined
2. Line the air fryer with parchment paper and spray with cooking spray
3. Preheat the air fryer to 200ºC
4. Dip each cookie in the pancake mix and place in the air fryer
5. Cook for 5 minutes, turn and cook for a further 3 minutes
6. Sprinkle with icing sugar to serve

Appendix : Recipes Index

A

Air Fried Maple Chicken Thighs 31
Air Fried Scallops 47
Air Fryer Chicken Thigh Schnitzel 38
Air Fryer Corn On The Cob 59
Air Fryer Mussels 44
Air Fryer Pork Bratwurst 24
Air Fryer Sesame Chicken Thighs 33
Air-fried Artichoke Hearts 56
Air-fried Pickles 15
Alternative Stuffed Potatoes 58
Apple And Cinnamon Puff Pastry Pies 68
Artichoke Crostini 50
Asian Devilled Eggs 15
Asian Meatballs 23
Aubergine Parmesan 59
Aubergine Parmigiana 53
Avocado Fries 6

B

Baba Ganoush 13
Bacon Smokies 20
Baked Feta, Tomato & Garlic Pasta 55
Bbq Chicken Tenders 30
Beef And Cheese Empanadas 29
Beef Stroganoff 22
Beef Wellington 25
Beetroot Crisps 17
Brazilian Pineapple 68
Breaded Pork Chops 27
Breakfast “pop Tarts” 12
Breakfast Doughnuts 6
Brownies 67
Butter Cake 70
Butternut Squash 60

C

Celery Root Fries 63
Cheese & Ham Sliders 24
Cheese Scones 11
Cheesy Meatballs 22

Cheesy Taco Crescents 14
Chicken & Bacon Parcels 17
Chicken & Potatoes 37
Chicken And Cheese Chimichangas 36
Chicken Fajitas 35
Chicken Kiev 35
Chicken Milanese 34
Chicken Tikka 32
Chicken Tikka Masala 39
Chocolate Cake 64
Chocolate Eclairs 66
Chocolate Orange Muffins 65
Chocolate-glazed Banana Slices 67
Christmas Biscuits 64
Coconut Shrimp 46
Cod Nuggets 41
Coffee, Chocolate Chip, And Banana Bread 66
Copycat Fish Fingers 42
Cornflake Chicken Nuggets 33
Courgette Burgers 55
Courgette Fries 5
Crispy Broccoli 62
Crispy Sweet & Spicy Cauliflower 58
Crunchy Chicken Tenders 31
Crunchy Fish 48
Cumin Shoestring Carrots 7

D

Delicious Breakfast Casserole 5

E

Easy Omelette 11
Egg & Bacon Breakfast Cups 6
Egg Fried Rice 60

F

Falafel Burgers 54
Fish Taco Cauliflower Rice Bowls 45
Flat Mushroom Pizzas 51
Focaccia Bread 18
French Toast Slices 8
Furikake Salmon 42

G

Garlic And Parsley Potatoes 62

Garlic Parmesan Fried Chicken Wings 32
Gnocchi Caprese 54
Granola 70
Grilled Ginger & Coconut Pineapple Rings 72

H

Halloumi Fries 7
Hard Boiled Eggs Air Fryer Style 10
Hasselback New Potatoes 57
Honey Roasted Parsnips 61

I

Italian Meatballs 26

J

Jackfruit Taquitos 49
Jalapeño Pockets 19
Jalapeño Poppers 19

K

Korean Chicken Wings 16

L

Lamb Burgers 26
Lamb Calzone 23
Lobster Tails 40

M

Macaroni & Cheese Quiche 51
Meaty Egg Cups 10
Mexican Breakfast Burritos 8
Mexican Rice 63
Milk And White Chocolate Chip Air Fryer Donuts With Frosting 69
Mini Calzones 16
Muhammara 9
Mushroom Pasta 52
Mustard Glazed Pork 28
Mustard Pork Tenderloin 26

N

New York Cheesecake 71

O

Oat & Parmesan Crusted Fish Fillets 40
Onion Bahji 21
Orange Sesame Cauliflower 61

P

Pao De Queijo 17
Parmesan Truffle Oil Fries 53
Pasta Chips 21
Peanut Butter And Banana Bites 67
Peppery Lemon Shrimp 45
Pistachio Brownies 71
Pizza Chicken Nuggets 34
Polenta Fries 13
Pork Belly With Crackling 24
Pork With Chinese 5 Spice 29
Potato & Chorizo Frittata 9
Pretzel Bites 19
Pulled Pork, Bacon, And Cheese Sliders 27
Pumpkin Fries 61

R

Radish Hash Browns 56
Rainbow Vegetables 55
Ranch Style Fish Fillets 41
Roast Cauliflower & Broccoli 49
Roast Pork 25
Roast Vegetables 50
Roasted Cauliflower 53
Roasted Okra 60

S

Satay Tofu Skewers 56
Scotch Eggs 18
Sea Bass With Asparagus Spears 43
Shrimp Wrapped With Bacon 47
Southern Style Pork Chops 23
Special Oreos 72
Spiced Apples 69
Spicy Chicken Wing Drummettes 36
Spicy Chickpeas 21
Steak Fajitas 28
Steak Popcorn Bites 25
Sticky Chicken Tikka Drumsticks 37
Stuffing Filled Pumpkin 57
Sugar Dough Dippers 65

Super Easy Fries 59
Sweet Potato Fries 7

T

Tandoori Salmon 48
Tex Mex Hash Browns 62
Thai Bites 20
Thai Fish Cakes 41
Thai Salmon Patties 46
Thai Turkey Burgers 30
Thai-style Tuna Fishcakes 44
Tilapia Fillets 43
Tomato And Herb Tofu 52
Tortellini Bites 14
Traditional Fish And Chips 40
Turkey Cutlets In Mushroom Sauce 34

W

Waffle Fries 20
Whole Chicken 38
Whole Wheat Pizza 51

Y

Yorkshire Puddings 58
Your Favourite Breakfast Bacon 12

Z

Zebra Cake 72
Zingy Brussels Sprouts 57